PSL MODEL RAILWAY GUIDE

5

Operating your layout

Michael Andress

PSL Patrick Stephens, Cambridge

Softbound edition first published March 1981

Combined casebound edition (with *PSL Model Railway Guide 6*) first published May 1983

British Library Cataloguing in Publication Data

Andress, Michael
  PSL model railway guide.
  5: Operating your layout
  1. Railroads — Models
  I. Title
  II. Model railway guide
  625.1'9   TF197

  ISBN 0-85059-436-7 (softbound)
  ISBN 0-85059-618-1 (combined casebound)

Cover photograph by Brian Monaghan

Text photoset in 8 on 9 pt Univers by Manuset Limited, Baldock, Herts.
Printed in Great Britain on 100 gsm Huntsman Velvet, and bound, by The Garden City Press, Letchworth, Herts, for the publishers Patrick Stephens Limited, Bar Hill, Cambridge, CB3 8EL, England.

Also in the same series and by the same author
1 Baseboards, track and electrification
2 Layout planning
3 Structure modelling
4 Scenery
6 Branch line railways
7 Modern railways
8 Narrow gauge railways

Contents

Introduction	5
The train set	6
Aims and advantages of operation	11
Branch line operation	13
Traffic on your railway	16
Prototype timetables	22
Compiling a simple timetable	23
Time and the speeded-up clock	33
The train graph	37
Bell codes	40
Card order systems	41
Loading and unloading	44
Maintenance	48
Exhibiting your layout	56

Introduction

The construction of a model railway layout can give the builder a great deal of enjoyment and satisfaction, but this is by no means all that the hobby has to offer. Operation of the completed layout in a realistic manner, following the principles of real railway practice, can provide continuing interest and entertainment for the enthusiast and his or her friends. Many modellers never realise the full potential of this aspect of the hobby and their running is merely haphazard. My aim in this book is to show the beginner how even a small and simple model railway can be operated in an interesting and realistic manner. There are various methods of running a model railway and we will look at the basic principles of some of these so that you can choose the one most suitable for you and your layout.

If the modeller is to gain the maximum pleasure from operating his layout it is essential that the model railway should run smoothly and reliably. For a layout to operate properly regular maintenance and repairs are required. Many beginners are uncertain just how to go about keeping their layouts and equipment in good order, and also feel that such work is likely to be a tedious chore anyway. However, for the most part, simple care and maintenance that you can easily carry out yourself is all that

is needed and I will cover these basic procedures in this book.

Participation in model railway exhibitions and shows can be a very enjoyable and satisfying activity for the enthusiast but also demands careful preparation for the most successful results. In the final section of this book I want to give the beginner some suggestions regarding this preparation and also about attendance and actual operation at the exhibitions themselves.

I would like to thank all those modellers who have kindly allowed me to use pictures of their models and layouts to illustrate this book. In particular I am grateful to Harold Bowcott, members of the Brooklands Railway Society Model Group, Allan Downes, members of the Greenwich & District Narrow Gauge Railway Group, Brian Monaghan, Bob Petch and Dick Wyatt. I am especially indebted to Chris Ellis for permission to include the description of how he compiled a timetable for his N-scale layout and to Geoff Barlow for his advice on maintenance and repairs. I am also grateful to those manufacturers who have provided information and pictures of their products, and particularly to Matt Ascough of M & R (Model Railways) Ltd for his assistance with information on the Fleischmann hump yard.

Left *Modern railway operation is a complex business but is built up from many simple train movements. In the same way model railway operation should be kept simple at first and developed later as experience is gained.*

The train set

The gift or purchase of a train set is the introduction to railway modelling for many enthusiasts and it is probably a good place for us to begin in considering model railway operation. With the basic train set oval the scope for operation is very limited indeed. We can run a train clockwise or anti-clockwise around the oval, we can stop it, start it and reverse it, and that is about all. Even if we place a station or two on the oval and use our imagination to pretend the train is running, say from London to Newcastle, with stops at various stations en route, the layout will not be very interesting to run. No matter how realistic the structures and scenery providing the setting for the railway are, the modeller will soon tire of the layout.

The operational interest and variety will be considerably increased by the addition of even two or three sidings as then we can carry out shunting duties. Trailing sidings are easily worked. The train stops short of the points and it is divided immediately behind the wagon or wagons intended for the siding. The engine and front part of the train then pulls forward over the points, these are changed and the train reverses on to the siding. The wagon or wagons for the siding are uncoupled and left there as the engine moves out of the siding on to the main line. The points are changed again and the engine backs up to reform the train. For a siding served by a facing point it is more difficult. The train stops short of the siding and is split immediately in front of the wagon or wagons for the siding. The engine must then run right round the oval to reach the rear of the train. The siding point is changed and the locomotive then pushes the train on to the siding. The wagon or wagons for the siding are uncoupled and left there while the engine pulls the remainder of the train out of the siding on to the main line again. The point is changed and the locomotive must again run right round the oval, this time to reach the front of the train once more. Normally when a train is made up wagons destined for the same siding will be placed together but, if for any reason they have not been, then further moves will be required to sort them out at the siding. Similarly, if there are one or more wagons to be collected by the train from the siding this will add to the movements needed as they must be removed

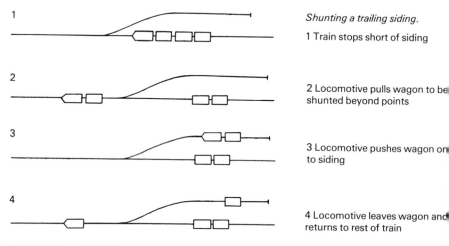

Shunting a trailing siding.

1 Train stops short of siding

2 Locomotive pulls wagon to be shunted beyond points

3 Locomotive pushes wagon on to siding

4 Locomotive leaves wagon and returns to rest of train

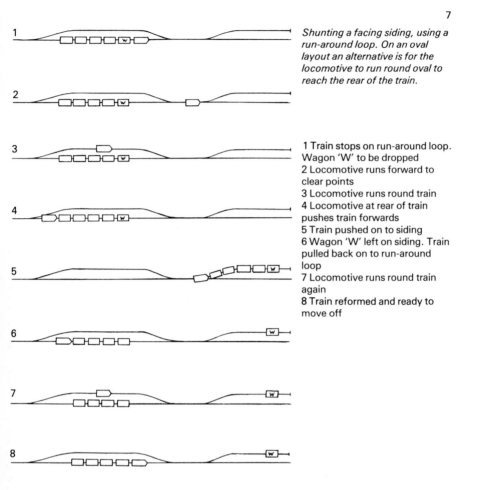

1 *Shunting a facing siding, using a run-around loop. On an oval layout an alternative is for the locomotive to run round oval to reach the rear of the train.*

1 Train stops on run-around loop. Wagon 'W' to be dropped
2 Locomotive runs forward to clear points
3 Locomotive runs round train
4 Locomotive at rear of train pushes train forwards
5 Train pushed on to siding
6 Wagon 'W' left on siding. Train pulled back on to run-around loop
7 Locomotive runs round train again
8 Train reformed and ready to move off

Placing two industries on one siding adds to the traffic and to the number of moves required in shunting. To shunt vans to warehouse, wagons at factory must be removed then replaced.

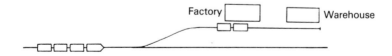

A kick-back siding also increases the shunting moves needed. To shunt wagons on to kick-back siding serving factory warehouse, siding must first be cleared.

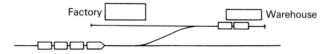

The train set

Above *The addition of a run-around loop and a siding to the basic oval makes it possible to run two trains on the layout, though not simultaneously, and to carry out a little shunting, as on this small simple layout built by Terry Jenkins.* **Below** *Here a Mainline 0-6-0 Tank Engine shunts the goods siding on Terry Jenkins' small layout.* **Right** *If a run-around loop is added to the basic train set oval the engine can reach the rear of the train for reversing direction. It also makes the shunting of facing sidings more convenient.*

om the siding before the arriving wagons are
hunted on to the track. Further complications
rise if one siding serves two different facilities
r industries. In this case a wagon at the nearer
ne may have to be temporarily removed to
llow access to a wagon further along the
ding, and then replaced in position at the
onclusion of the shunting. If there is a fan of
dings, a set of two or more sidings from a
ngle lead from the main line, then there is
dditional scope for sorting of the arriving
agons. We can provide various facilities, a
oods shed, a cattle dock, coal staithes and so
n, for these sidings, adding to the interest and
e appearance. A kick-back siding is a track
ading off, in the reverse direction, from
nother siding. Because the main siding must
e cleared to allow the locomotive to shunt the
ick-back siding such an arrangement adds to
e number of shunting movements required.
ome modellers find this a nuisance and hence
o not bother to shunt the kick-back siding.
Iowever, if you like shunting, and particularly
your layout is small and thus needs as much
perating potential as possible in what space is
vailable, you may benefit from including one
r more sidings of this type on it. An advantage
f such sidings is that they enable you to place
xtra tracks in situations where the space could
ot otherwise be utilised for sidings.

With a simple oval layout with sidings it is
ossible to accommodate two trains, one on
he main line and the other stored on a siding,
hough they cannot both be run at the same
me. The provision of a run-around or passing
oop will make shunting more convenient and
vill add to the operational flexibility. To reverse
he train it is stopped on one track of the loop,
lear of both points, and the locomotive is
ncoupled and run ahead to clear the points. It
s then moved back along the other track past
he train and over the points behind the train.
he engine is then advanced to be coupled to
he rear of the train. If it is a goods train with a
uards van to be transferred as well as the
ngine, then additional moves will be required.
imilarly, when shunting a siding served by a
acing point the locomotive can run round the
oop to reach the rear of the train and does not
eed to travel right round the oval. A passing
oop also makes it more convenient to operate
wo trains on a small oval layout, as one can be
eld on one track of the loop while the other
ravels around the main line, using the other
rack of the passing loop to go by the
tationary train. When desired the moving train
an be stopped on the loop track and the other
rain can be run on the main line. Again, only
ne train can be in action at once.

On a point to point layout the provision of a

passing loop at an intermediate station will allow trains running in opposite directions to pass at the station, and will also facilitate shunting. At a small terminus a run-around loop is almost always provided so that the locomotive of an arriving train can move round to the other end of the train for the return journey. The presence of the loop also means that both facing and trailing sidings can be shunted. Often the loop is made up by including a release crossover between two tracks and the loop is frequently positioned alongside the platform or platforms saving space on the layout. However, it can alternatively be placed before the platform where it may be more convenient for goods trains, which usually share the same run-around loop at small stations. In this case, the passenger trains will be reversed on to the loop after arrival for the engine to run round and then return to the platform to await departure.

With this arrangement it is easy, if you wish, to provide separate arrival and departure tracks and platforms. Push-pull or auto-trains, railcars and multiple units do not, of course, require a run-around loop as they can operate equally well in either direction. Occasionally at small termini, and often on the platform roads at larger termini, no release crossover is provided. In this situation the arriving train, after the passengers have left, is uncoupled from the locomotive and is then pulled away to the carriage sidings by another engine, often the station pilot. Once the coaches have been removed the original train locomotive moves away to the engine servicing area. Except at small stations a head shunt is usually provided. This is a track parallel to the main line and linked to the sidings so that a locomotive can shunt the goods sidings without the need to use the main line; thus the latter is left clear for trains arriving at and departing from the station.

If we have double track on our oval or point to point line then it becomes easy to run two trains simultaneously, but in many ways operation is more interesting with the difficulties imposed by using single track with passing loops. The need to time train movements correctly so that the trains can pass each other at the loops with the minimum of delay will add to the interest. Thus, even with a simple layout built up from a train set we can carry out most of the basic train movements. Though many of these are straightforward the beginner does need to familiarise himself with the correct methods. He will also find that, with practice, he will become more adept and efficient, both at carrying out the actual movements and also at planning his shunting so that the minimum number of moves will be required. He will also become skilled at running his locomotives smoothly and at a realistic speed while shunting.

These moves, though an essential part of running a model railway, are the 'how' rather than the 'why' of operation. Having considered some of the details of train movements we can now look at the aims of operation.

Aims and advantages of operation

For some modellers the great interest in the hobby comes from the construction. They may enjoy all types of this work or may tend to specialise in one or more aspects, for example, trackwork, scenery or locomotives. For them the enjoyment comes with building the layout and, in many cases, once the work is essentially completed, they lose much of their enthusiasm. They may run a few trains in a rather haphazard manner, but are soon planning extensions, alterations or even a new layout. Now, of course, railway modelling is a hobby and it is up to the individual how he wishes to enjoy it. Indeed, one of the great advantages of this hobby is the very wide range of different activities which it offers. However, I do feel that many beginners who successfully construct layouts with much enjoyment and entertainment in the process are then rather uncertain of what to do with the completed model. They run trains in a random manner, in train set fashion, and are unaware of the great potential for entertainment that model railway operation can offer. Indeed, for some enthusiasts, construction of a layout, though satisfying in itself, is really just a means to an end — the operation of the layout. These modellers have created a fascinating form of game, with the entertainment value of a complex board game, but with the added attraction of seeing authentic models in action in a realistic scenic setting. One of the American pioneers in model railway operation, the late Frank Ellison, likened the operation of a layout to the presentation of a play in a theatre and certainly the running of some of the large and complex model railroads in the United States, by teams of skilled operators, can be a dramatic and exciting performance.

Already we have seen that, even on a small oval layout of the type easily developed from a train set, running a train, especially a goods train, can involve us in a considerable number of train movements. However, interesting though they can be, the movements I have described are really only the mechanics of how we handle the train once we have decided when and where that train will run.

For operation which will remain interesting and entertaining on a model railway layout, we must base it as realistically as possible on the way in which prototype railways are run. The aim of the real railways is to transport people and goods as efficiently and economically as possible, within the limitations imposed by safety regulations and any commitments with regard to services they are obliged to provide, even though they may be unprofitable. Obviously there are limitations, particularly due to lack of space, on our layouts but, as far as possible, our trains should reproduce the operation of the real ones. Thus our trains should appear to have a purpose when they move and not just look as if they are running haphazardly, as the whim of the operator takes them. On the prototype, goods vehicles are moved according to the needs of the customers and we must be sure that we distribute our rolling stock in a realistic manner representing the transport of goods between customers.

Thus what we require is some system or scheme of operating which will give the impression that our trains are travelling around the layout in the same way as prototype trains on the real railways. Generally, the best results will come from using a system based on or adapted from prototype operation. Because of this some familiarity with prototype practice is beneficial and, indeed, finding out more about how the real thing runs can be very interesting in itself as well as helping you to operate your own layout more realistically.

Various methods have been devised by different modellers to suit their own layouts and the type of operation which interests them most. The majority of these schemes are based either on timetable, or sequence, operation, on some system of rolling stock distribution, or on a combination of both. Later in this book we will look at some of the possibilities that you could employ on your model railway.

Now you may be thinking that the idea of prototype-based operation and the use of a timetable is all very well on a large and complex

A small branch line terminus beautifully modelled in 4 mm scale by Allan Downes. All the structures were scratch-built. Such a station provides a good introduction to model railway operation but the scope is somewhat limited as prototype branch lines usually run rather restricted timetables. (Photograph by Brian Monaghan.)

layout with several operators, but that it is not relevant for a small and simple one-man model railway. However, this is not so and, even on a small oval layout, such as might be developed from a train set, it is perfectly feasible to run a timetable or sequence operation scheme. Admittedly, some imagination is required. For example, the journey is often made up of a number of laps of the circuit and we must ignore the fact that the train keeps passing the same features on each lap of the track. However, a model railway can never be an exact replica of the real thing so we must always use some imagination; indeed it is part of the fun to do so. An example of how interesting operation can be provided by a

minimum space layout is given by a 3 feet by 2 feet N-gauge layout recently built by Chris Ellis. Despite the small size and simple track plan, a realistic and entertaining schedule has been devised. In a later section in this book Chris Ellis explains how he drew up the timetable and the reasoning behind it.

It was the search for greater realism in railway modelling despite limited space and other resources that encouraged the development of the concept of branch line modelling. Because the branch line model railway forms a good introduction to operation, and in fact to scale railway modelling in general, I would like to consider the subject in more detail.

Branch line operation

If we are to have a realistic model railway in a small space with a necessarily simple track plan we must select a suitable prototype — the country branch line in the days of steam is an ideal choice. Trains often consisted of only two or three coaches or a few wagons pulled by a small tank engine and the station track layouts were usually fairly simple.

During the 1950s the branch line model railway concept was developed considerably. At that time the idea was not so much to provide a suitable subject for beginners as to enable more experienced workers to create a model railway which was realistic in appearance and operation in a small space. The short prototype trains allowed the modeller to run authentic length trains despite the small size of the layout. Also, because the station track layouts were simple on branch lines, they can be compressed to fit on to a model railway while still keeping their essential features. Thus the model can be operated according to prototype practice and following a proper timetable.

The aim was not to make an exact scale model of a particular branch line station; even the simple stations on country branches occupied a considerable ground area and would take too much space on a layout if reproduced accurately to scale. If space for this was available it would be better utilised in modelling a more complex and more interesting station with greater operating potential. In fact, though some enthusiasts have been very successful in basing their branch line stations closely on particular prototypes, many modellers find that it suits them better to combine features from a variety of real stations to produce an interesting and attractive model with all the features they want.

To reiterate then, the key points are having realistic trains operating in an authentic manner. The advantage of branch line stations is that their simple track plans, with few points, permit considerable selective compression without affecting the essential features which influence the way the station can be operated.

Because the aim was realistic operation, the point to point track arrangement was usually preferred to the continuous run schemes, and the now classic branch line terminus to fiddle yard (hidden sidings representing the rest of the system) design was developed. Such a track plan can be fitted on to baseboards of various shapes but a popular arrangement is on two narrow baseboards in an L shape, often fitted into the corner of a room. This design has the advantage of providing the greatest running possibilities in a minimum area and often a layout of this shape can be fitted into a room whereas a conventional rectangular baseboard would not be acceptable as it would block the centre of the room too much.

A branch line layout of this type is also very

A branch line layout can be the ideal introduction to model railway operation for the beginner.

Branch line operation

Above *Bob Petch's 00-gauge layout features a GWR branch line through station, Limpley, with a fiddle yard at each end of the line to complete the layout. Here a milk train has been held in the loop at the station to allow a mineral train to pass. Modelling a through station enables the operator to run traffic on the line for which there are no facilities at the station, giving greater scope than with a terminus. This photograph was taken at an exhibition; note the chairs at top right employed to keep the viewers clear of the model.*

Left *One of the two fiddle yards on Bob Petch's layout. Note the sheet of instructions for the fiddle yard operator at bottom right of the picture.*

uitable for the beginner. Now that so many high quality ready-made items such as track, ocomotives and rolling stock are available at ery reasonable prices such a layout can quickly be brought to a stage where it is nteresting to view and operate. The good quality of the commercial items means that, with reasonable care, even the beginner should achieve satisfactory running and be able to enjoy organised operation. It is also easy to add structures and scenery to give an attractive appearance.

The terminus to fiddle yard scheme lends itself very well to authentic operation, based either on a prototype timetable or on one devised by the modeller to suit his own stock and interests. Prototype branch line timetables were usually simple and were often operated on the 'one engine in steam' principle so there is no reason why the beginner with only one locomotive and a limited selection of rolling stock should not be able to run his layout in a realistic manner. The fiddle yard represents the rest of the branch and the junction station. Here trains are made up by hand, without worrying about any pretence of realism and are then despatched to the terminus station where any necessary shunting or other train movements are carried out in an authentic and realistic manner. The train then returns to the fiddle yard. The terminus can operate realistically following the timetable and dealing with all the trains from the imaginary junction.

Such a line is an excellent introduction to operation for the newcomer as it will get him started without difficulty. As he gains experience and additional rolling stock he can extend the basic timetable to make it more fun to operate. The disadvantage is that traffic on a prototype branch line was rather limited in scope and extent and, if the model is to be realistic, operation on it must necessarily also be relatively restricted. Running too intensive a service on a model branch line will destroy the illusion of realism which we are trying to create. Because of these limitations the modeller is likely to find that, in time, he loses interest and will then need to extend the layout or even scrap it and change to a larger system.

Though the classic terminus to fiddle yard scheme described above is the most popular design, there is an interesting alternative arrangement which was, I believe, first employed by Maurice Deane. This is to fit the branch line on a rectangular baseboard with a central operating well and with the line curved round so that the fiddle yard is behind the terminus, concealed by a low backscene. This has the advantage that the modeller working alone can easily reach both the terminus and the fiddle yard beyond it from his operating position in the central well. It also makes it easy to include a link to create an oval so that continuous running is possible if desired. The link can be concealed so that the realism of the point to point scheme is not impaired.

Another idea in which there has been more interest recently, perhaps partly to provide a change from the usual design, is the modelling of a through station on a branch line rather than the terminus. Such an arrangement can be operated as an oval with hidden sidings on the side opposite to the through station, or as a point to point design with a fiddle yard at each end, a reversing loop at each end or with a fiddle yard at one end and a reversing loop at the other, making up an out and back arrangement. The choice of a through station does have certain advantages, particularly in allowing greater scope for traffic on the line.

Branch line operation

Traffic on your railway

Before we can plan a timetable or schedule for a layout we must have some idea of the traffic it should carry. The prototype railways, of course, must cope with whatever traffic they are offered. Passengers wish to travel from town to town, commercial and industrial customers want goods and freight transferred to and from their factories, warehouses and depots, and so on. Trains are run to handle these demands and the make up of these trains may be adjusted from day to day and from season to season according to variations in the traffic.

Now if we are modelling a specific station or are basing our layout on a particular line, more or less closely, then the type of traffic will largely be determined for us. From the working timetable of the prototype, if it is available, from details about the line in books and magazine articles, and from a knowledge of the nature of the countryside served by the railway, we can build up an accurate picture of the traffic the line would carry. If we have, on the other hand, created our own station and line we must also develop a background for it. We may choose to base it on a particular area and we can then follow the general traffic trends for lines in the part of the country concerned. Alternatively, we may wish to create our own imaginary countryside for the railway to run through.

Whatever course we choose, it is important to build up a background picture of this sort if we are to have a realistic pattern of traffic for the layout. The branch line again serves as a useful example, partly because it is a good subject for a beginner's first scale layout, and

partly because the simple timetable of the prototype makes a good introduction to model railway operation. Let us consider the small branch line terminus first of all. It is likely to be in a country area or serving a small coastal port or seaside town. If we model a terminus station then traffic on our layout from the fiddle yard to the terminus must stop there. All movements on the layout should have a purpose, if our operating is to appear realistic, so wagons will only be moved from the fiddle yard to the terminus and back if there is freight to be carried to or from the station. As the station is a terminus, the type of rolling stock on the line will be limited by the traffic handling facilities at the station. For example, if we have no cattle dock then we cannot run cattle wagons, and so on. If you find this unduly limiting you may prefer to model a through station. This is much less restricting regarding the rolling stock we operate on the line as we can always say that stock for which there are no facilities at the station is merely en route to other destinations further along the line!

Coming back to our small terminus we can first of all consider the passenger traffic. We will need a train early in the morning to take people from the small town to work at the junction town or at other places along the main line from there (all represented by the fiddle yard) and a train to bring them back in the late afternoon or early evening. A train going later in the morning and one back during the afternoon will provide a service for shoppers while a train each way in the evening will cope with passengers wanting to spend an evening at the cinema or at other entertainments in the

Top right *This wooden extension to the platform was provided for milk traffic at Watlington and has been faithfully reproduced on the Mid Hants Model Railway Group model of the station.* **Above right** *The Mid Hants Model Railway Group's accurate model of Watlington station, an Oxfordshire branch line terminus, in EM gauge. This picture shows part of the goods yard which has facilities typical of a small country station. The beautifully detailed goods shed was scratch-built by Barry Fisher. The track on the right is used for coal wagons and storage.* **Right** *Typical traffic at a country branch line station includes livestock and farm equipment as seen here on the EM-gauge model of Watlington station. Note the many small details which add interest and realism to the scene.*

Traffic on your railway

Above *A Hornby 0-6-0 Pannier Tank Engine and an auto-coach made up from a BSL kit form this typical auto-train seen at Stonepark Lane, an 00-gauge country branch line terminus. Because these trains run in either direction the engine does not need to run round the train at the terminus.* **Above right** *Livestock was an important part of the goods traffic on many branch lines and the pens at Corfe Castle station on the 00-gauge model of the Swanage branch, built by the Isle of Purbeck Model Railway Club, contain cattle, sheep and pigs.* **Right** *The provision of industrial sidings will add greatly to the scope and interest of operation. On Harold Bowcott's 00-gauge layout, sidings serve this large factory and the hopper for the transfer of minerals from the narrow-gauge line at the left of the picture.* (Photograph by Brian Monaghan.)

larger town. Some of these services can be by push-pull train or a railcar but these involve less movements as no running round by the engine is required. Therefore it is best to have some of the services provided by ordinary trains so that there will be more shunting. Extra trains will be needed on Saturdays and on market days. If we place our terminus at a seaside or holiday resort then we will need more trains in the summer and may run through coaches or even through trains from London or other cities for the holiday visitors. In rural areas we may need additional trains for seasonal workers depending on the crops grown in the district. Thus variety can be introduced in the passenger traffic for even a fairly small terminus.

When we look at the freight side there is even more scope. Domestic coal was an important item in the days of the steam-operated branch line and our station should have a siding with coal staithes for this traffic. In addition, if we base a locomotive at the

terminus with a small engine shed and water tower we will need to provide coal for it and this will make up extra coal traffic on the line.

In a rural area much of the freight traffic will be related to agriculture. This may be crops, grain, vegetables or fruit which will need to be shipped out. Incoming traffic will include fertilisers and occasionally farm equipment such as a plough or tractor. The area may be more concerned with livestock so that we need to provide a cattle dock or sheep pens at our terminus, together with appropriate rolling stock to transport the animals. If horses are to be carried we will need one or more horse boxes on our rolling stock roster. Animal feed shipped in will further add to the traffic. There will also be goods coming in for the shops and the local pub, together with items ordered by people living in the town or village and on nearby farms.

If we have room for a dairy, a small sawmill or a quarry we can introduce suitable extra rolling stock to handle this special traffic; the

additional operational scope will also increase the interest. However, we should not run any stock for which there is clearly no traffic being generated if we are to maintain the realism. If we have chosen a small port as the setting for our terminus we can introduce fish traffic with a special fish train running through to the junction or beyond. There may also be goods brought to the dock for shipment in coastal freighters.

We may have space for a larger station and this will enable us to include more facilities and to introduce more types of traffic, making both the selection of rolling stock and the scope of operation more interesting. The terminus would be serving a larger town and we can probably provide some light industry. This will require incoming raw materials and perhaps coal as fuel, and there will be finished goods to be shipped out.

No hard and fast rules need be laid down regarding the traffic. The important thing is for there to be visible facilities and reasons for the traffic and that it should be appropriate to the area and to the type of community that your station serves. It is useful to decide on this sort of background to your line before planning the traffic and timetable so that you are quite clear just what your aims are. Otherwise you may be tempted to add this and that and to acquire unsuitable rolling stock, resulting in an unrealistic overall effect.

The whole concept can be approached in

Traffic on your railway

Above Motorail services are now widely available in Britain and Europe. These two pictures show the facility at Narbonne on the SNCF. Special services of this type can be an interesting addition to model railway operation. **Below** Such services are often not exclusive to the contemporary scene. Here we see 'Motorail' Victorian style modelled on Mike Sharman's 4 mm scale period layout!

various ways. One method is to decide on the location and type of line and to build up a picture of the sort of traffic pattern the railway should have. The layout can then be designed to fit in with this. Alternatively you can start with an already completed layout plan, perhaps a published design, and then plan out from this a traffic pattern which would be appropriate for the facilities provided. If you work from a prototype track plan, such as often appear in magazines and books, you can carry out a similar exercise but you will also have additional information available about the line and the area in which it was situated to help create a realistic and authentic operating scheme.

Once we have decided on the sort of traffic our line will carry we will have a good idea of the type of trains we will be running and of the rolling stock required. For the amount of traffic, most modellers use prototype lines of a similar nature as a guide or, if they are copying a particular prototype, they follow the pattern of that line. Often country branch lines had very simple timetables with relatively few trains, and modellers may wish to introduce a little more activity with a few extra trains, though this must not be overdone or the character of the model will be distorted. Even if your station serves an imaginary town you can work out the amount of traffic which would be likely by using real towns of a similar size as a guide. For example, David Jenkinson calculated the daily wagon movements for cattle, coal, minerals, milk and general goods stock on his Marthwaite layout using statistics from Settle and Carlisle stations as a basis. His excellent description appeared in the December 1966 issue of *Railway Modeller* magazine and gives a good example of how the traffic pattern for a model railway layout can be logically built up to give a realistic and authentic operating scheme.

Once we have a clear idea of the traffic our line will carry, we can go on to produce a schedule or timetable setting out the details of how our trains will run. Before devising a timetable for our layout it is perhaps a good time to look briefly at the real thing.

Traffic on your railway

Prototype timetables

The railway timetables with which everyone is familiar are the public timetables which cover only the passenger train schedules listing only their times for the stations at which they stop. Much more useful for the railway modeller interested in operation are the working timetables, issued to employees of the railway. These list all trains on the line concerned, passenger and freight, with their timings and with many other details such as train numbers and classification, speed restrictions, information regarding stops for shunting, for other trains to pass, and so on. These timetables are private and not for publication or general distribution. However, many are available unofficially in railway enthusiast circles

and a number, mainly from steam days, have been published. For example, The Oxford Railway Publishing Company Ltd can offer Cambrian Railway (1904), Somerset & Dorset Railway (1920), Southern Railway (West Division) (1932) and Southern Railway (Isle of Wight) (1932) Passenger and Working Timetables, and more timetable reprints are to be published in due course. Many books on particular branch lines include details of their working timetables and these are invaluable to modellers building layouts based on these lines. The excellent books *Great Western Branch Line Termini* Vols 1 & 2 by Paul Karau, published by The Oxford Railway Publishing Company, for example, include working timetables for the branches concerned and also very useful details on how the termini were operated. Even if you are not modelling one of these lines the timetables would be a useful guide if you are operating a branch line layout.

If the modeller has chosen a specific branch, either to model exactly or as a general basis for his layout and he can obtain the working timetable for the period he wishes to model then there will be no difficulty in running an accurate timetable service. As mentioned earlier familiarity with the economy of the area modelled and with the type of traffic the branch carried will enable him to realistically represent operation on the line. If it is not possible to find a copy of the authentic timetable it is still possible to devise a reasonable schedule from the track plan, station facilities and from what is known of the general type and extent of the traffic. Alternatively a timetable from a similar branch could be employed, perhaps with modifications to suit the needs of the modeller.

Left *Working timetables are issued to employees and give much more information than the ordinary public timetables, making them especially useful for railway modellers interested in operation.*

Compiling a simple timetable

Having considered the type of traffic we will have on our line, and perhaps with some prototype timetables to guide us, we can tackle the job of producing our first simple timetable. It is important not to try to devise anything too complicated at first as it is easy to become confused by too many details even though the principles may be straightforward. Because of its simplicity a branch line terminus timetable makes a good beginning. Again as branch line timetables were often very simple, frequently such lines operated on the one engine in steam principle, they can be conveniently carried out in model form using the sequence method. This type of running is well suited to the beginner to model railway operation and is also

especially suitable for one modeller operating on his own, as is often likely to be the case with a small branch line layout.

Sequence operation is a simple but orderly pattern of operation which overcomes the difficulty that, with a simple timetable (such as would apply to a small branch line terminus or through station) there will be long time intervals between trains. Because of this there are likely to be periods when the operator has nothing to do for some minutes, even when using a speeded-up clock system. With sequence operation a list of train movements is drawn up, as with an ordinary timetable, but these are carried out in simple sequence without regard to the time. Once one move-

A simple timetable.
SX = Except Sunday. **SO** = Sunday only. **Auto** = Auto Train. **Pass** = Passenger.

DOWN TRAINS	PASS	AUTO SO	AUTO SX	MIXED SX	AUTO SO	PASS	AUTO	AUTO
	am	am	am	am	pm	pm	pm	pm
FIDDLE YARD	7.30	9.40	9.55	11.30	1.06	5.10	6.30	8.35
HALT	7.38	9.48	10.03	11.46	1.14	5.18	6.38	8.48
TERMINUS	7.49	9.59	10.14	12.08	1.25	5.29	6.46	8.59

UP TRAINS	PASS	AUTO SO	AUTO SX	GOODS SX	AUTO SO	PASS	AUTO	AUTO
	am	am	am	pm	pm	pm	pm	pm
TERMINUS	8.02	10.20	10.30	1.04	1.35	5.40	7.00	9.05
HALT	8.13	10.31	10.41	1.26	1.46	5.51	7.11	9.16
FIDDLE YARD	8.21	10.41	10.49	1.42	1.54	5.59	7.19	9.24

Compiling a simple timetable

ment has taken place the operator goes on to the next. Thus it does not matter how quickly or slowly the enthusiast carries out the operations. If he wishes to pause he can do so, merely commencing again with the next train on the list. This is ideal for the beginner as he can get used to running the trains at realistic speeds and to carrying out shunting, also in a smooth and authentic manner, without being under any pressure to keep to time. And conversely there are no periods when he has nothing to do but wait. There is no reason why the modeller should not work through a prototype timetable using this system. Instead of sending out a train at, for example, 2.25 pm either by real or scale time, the train is despatched in its turn, and the time then is regarded as being 2.25 pm. Sequence operation, as I have mentioned previously, is particularly suited to operation of a simple layout, especially a branch line terminus or through station layout with one engine only running at any one time. Here there is not the need, as there may be on a larger more complex layout with two or more operators, for trains to pass or meet other trains or to clear trackage by a certain time. When there are more operators and there are trains which must interlock in their running we need some standard, most conveniently provided by all running to the same clock, whether speeded up or not, so that operation maintains an orderly pattern. Otherwise chaos may result.

As I have already indicated, sequence operation is particularly suitable for the single handed operator though it can still be used with two or more modellers. In this case they can all work from the same sequence card. Alternatively, they can work from cards of their own but provision must be made for keeping the sequence, either by exchanging cards between operators at the appropriate stages, or by including instructions that a particular movement must not be carried out until after the other operator has made some move.

Ideally at the end of the sequence all the stock should be back where it started so that the next sequence can begin. Generally, as with timetables, it is a good idea to begin with a simple limited sequence, then add to it as you gain experience and stock. If a particular sequence becomes boring after a time through repetition, then rearrange it to provide some variety. Extra interest can also be added by running some unscheduled trains such as a track repair train, a special passenger train, perhaps to bring people to an agricultural show, a seasonal goods train for a fruit crop, and so on.

To complete this section I would like to give you an example of how one modeller has created an interesting and realistic operating scheme for a very small layout. Chris Ellis recently built an N-gauge layout only 3 feet by 2 feet in size. He has described the construction of the layout in a series of articles in the magazine, *Model Train,* and I am most grateful for his permission to include here his working timetable and an outline, based on his description, of how he developed this timetable. His layout is based on an American prototype, the Chicago & North Western Railroad, but the basic principles are essentially similar to the making of a timetable for a British line.

The Warren, Beresford and Chicago Railroad was designed to provide interest in operation as well as in construction, and the operating concept of the layout was evolved as

Opposite and following three pages *Operation on the N-gauge American prototype Warren, Beresford and Chicago layout built by Chris Ellis.* (All photographs by Chris Ellis.) *1 An operator using the timetable alongside the controller. A Scoot is in the fiddle yard, at the rear centre of the picture, ready to run to Warren. 2 The Scoot moving along the fiddle yard siding heading up the branch to Warren. 3 Switching at North Warren. The Illinois Central reefer (refrigerated car) is being pulled out of the dairy siding. It will be put on the 'main line' and the Lackawanna boxcar will replace it at the dairy loading bank. The tank car will then go on to the Shell siding. 4 The Lackawanna boxcar is now being spotted at the dairy. 5 The branch freight approaching Warren headed by the Fairbanks-Morse H-12-44 switcher (Minitrix model repainted in Chicago and North Western colours). 6 Scoot (Train No 914) heading for Chicago (pushing) while the local freight is switched at North Warren. 7 Local mine train (No 910) arrives in the fiddle yard and is removed from the track. 8 Switching is suspended while Scoot No 913 arrives at the station at Warren. The local freight locomotive has gone to North Warren to lay over. 9 The Scoot has departed and the local freight locomotive arrives back at Warren to resume switching, bringing with it the cars picked up at North Warren. 10 Local freight locomotive laying over at North Warren while the Scoot occupies Warren station (see photo 8). 11 Switching the mine — Train No 909 changing loaded hoppers for the empties it has just brought in. Note the flagman on the road crossing. 12 Train No 912 — the local freight returning from Warren/North Warren to Chrystal Lake.*

4

5

6

7

8

9

10

11

12

follows. First of all, think in basic terms. What is the aim of the railroad? The answer is to carry people and goods from one point to another. Our layout is the most basic form of railway, a simple single track branch line doing exactly that, carrying goods and people from an 'off-stage' location (the equivalent of the fiddle yard on the classic branch line terminus type of layout) to the stations and depots on the board. From here it is a matter of choosing a location for the line. You can make up a completely mythical line with a 'company' name of its own if desired. Or you can do as we did and find a suitable railway to which your 'branch' can be connected as a fictional addition. The further alternative of modelling an actual location was not really practical for a small oval layout like this because there is insufficient space to represent it properly.

This led us to a 'fictional addition' to a real railway. We wanted a railway which would lend itself to a simple compact branch line, offer a busy service in real life, and enable us to use ready-to-run N-scale items with a minimum of adaptation. One line (but by no means the only one) which fitted these requirements was the Chicago North Western Railroad which operates out of Chicago, west and north-west as its name implies. This may seem somewhat exotic to some readers, but it is colourful in its snappy green/yellow paint scheme, it has a wide selection of motive power, it is a relatively small, tightly managed company, and it has lots of very rural country branch lines, almost as though the old Great Western Railway was still running its 1948 network in this modern diesel age. All the locomotives and stock required to operate a CNW layout are readily available in current N-gauge production, even though a little repainting and adaptation may be necessary. Above all, it operates a commuter service into Chicago which runs further out into the country than any of the other lines in the area with commuter service. Its route to the furthest commuter outpost, the holiday and residential resort of Lake Geneva, Wisconsin, is 73 miles by rail from Chicago on a branch of great charm and beauty.

By American standards the commuter trains offer a very frequent service, and these trains operated by double-decker (or bi-level) cars are short. So a branch line similar to the Lake Geneva branch offered us a modern era setting, with short trains, which could be dovetailed neatly into the existing network. The sketch map of the CNW routes, over which a commuter service operates, is included here and our branch is added to it, running to Warren (and North Warren—freight only) from Chrystal Lake. This new branch lends itself so

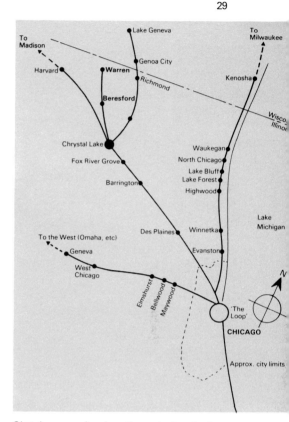

Sketch map showing the actual suburban routes from Chicago of the Chicago and North Western Railway system, with the addition of the fictional Warren branch coming off at Chrystal Lake. Only major stations are shown—there are actually more than 70 in the area of the map. Clybourn, mentioned on the train schedule, is the first junction out of Madison Street station in Chicago. (Courtesy Chris Ellis.)

well to existing CNW operations that we could readily produce a passenger schedule exactly like all other CNW leaflets you can pick up at stations on the line! If you do have access to a home printing set, it adds an amusing extra element to your layout if you have some realistic timetables to display and give to visitors.

A printed schedule, however, is really only the icing on the cake. It will impress your friends and help to bring the layout to life. To operate the layout with a logical schedule of runs you need something more mundane—a working timetable. Real timetables can appear very complicated and on a large model railway

Compiling a simple timetable

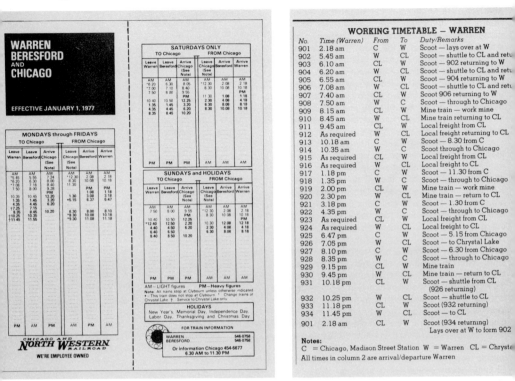

WORKING TIMETABLE – WARREN

No.	Time (Warren)	From	To	Duty/Remarks
901	2.18 am	C	W	Scoot — lays over at W
902	5.45 am	W	CL	Scoot — shuttle to CL and retu
903	6.10 am	CL	W	Scoot — 902 returning to W
904	6.20 am	W	CL	Scoot — shuttle to CL and retu
905	6.55 am	CL	W	Scoot — 904 returning to W
906	7.08 am	W	CL	Scoot — shuttle to CL and retu
907	7.40 am	CL	W	Scoot 906 returning to W
908	7.50 am	W	C	Scoot — through to Chicago
909	8.15 am	CL	W	Mine train — work mine
910	8.45 am	W	CL	Mine train returning to CL
911	9.45 am	CL	W	Local freight from CL
912	As required	W	CL	Local freight returning to CL
913	10.18 am	C	W	Scoot — 8.30 from C
914	10.35 am	W	C	Scoot through to Chicago
915	As required	CL	W	Local freight from CL
916	As required	W	CL	Local freight to CL
917	1.18 pm	C	W	Scoot — 11.30 from C
918	1.35 pm	W	C	Scoot — through to Chicago
919	2.00 pm	CL	W	Mine train — work mine
920	2.30 pm	W	CL	Mine train — return to CL
921	3.18 pm	C	W	Scoot — 1.30 from C
922	4.35 pm	W	C	Scoot — through to Chicago
923	As required	CL	W	Local freight from CL
924	As required	W	CL	Local freight to CL
925	6.47 pm	C	W	Scoot — 5.15 from Chicago
926	7.05 pm	W	CL	Scoot — to Chrystal Lake
927	8.10 pm	C	W	Scoot — 6.30 from Chicago
928	8.35 pm	W	C	Scoot — through to Chicago
929	9.15 pm	CL	W	Mine train
930	9.45 pm	W	CL	Mine train — return to CL
931	10.18 pm	CL	W	Scoot — shuttle from CL (926 returning)
932	10.25 pm	W	CL	Scoot — shuttle to CL
933	11.18 pm	CL	W	Scoot (932 returning)
934	11.45 pm	W	CL	Scoot — to CL
901	2.18 am	CL	W	Scoot (934 returning) Lays over at W to form 902

Notes:
C = Chicago, Madison Street Station   W = Warren   CL = Chrysta
All times in column 2 are arrival/departure Warren

Left *The train schedule for the Warren, Beresford and Chicago layout was reproduced to the exact size and style of the real CNW passenger timetables.* (Courtesy Chris Ellis.) **Right** *Working timetable for the Warren, Beresford and Chicago layout.* (Courtesy Chris Ellis.)

operation can be complex. However, here we have only the simplest of single line branches on which it is physically impossible to run more than one train at a time. Consequently, our timetable should be a simple one.

For a start, we forgot about time, real or speeded up, since ours is a layout for leisurely home operation and the pace of working is entirely up to you. Yes, there are nominated arrival and departure times for all the trains operating in a sequence throughout the day, but these times are descriptive rather than actual. Looking at the working timetable given here you will see that the first train in the 24 hour weekday schedule is the 2.18 am arrival in Warren from Chrystal Lake — representing the connecting train (at Chrystal Lake) with the last train of the day out of Chicago. So if you choose to start an operating session with this train it is simply the 2.18 am, no matter what time your operating session starts.

Obviously, to work this out we had to know some basic timings and make some

assumptions. So to start with we got hold of the train schedules for all the commuter runs on the CNW network. Using the train schedule for the Chicago-Harvard route (on which line is the all-important Chrystal Lake junction) it is easy enough to plot the frequency of passenger trains to and from the CNW station in Chicago. We made an early assumption here which was dictated by the limited trackage at Warren; because there are no spare sidings at Warren we could not have passenger trains 'laying over' waiting for their next turn. On the real railway, where most commuter runs are crowded into the morning or evening rush hours, the trains lay over in sidings in Chicago, Harvard, Chrystal Lake, etc, until they are next required for service. At Warren any such lay over would impede the running of freight trains, so incoming passenger trains are marked on the working timetable as returning to Chrystal Lake to lay over. A more likely alternative to this would be a siding 'off the board' beyond Beresford, where the train could be held until it returned to Warren for the next scheduled run to Chicago. At present this does not worry us—the train just runs back to siding A and is taken off the track until next required. If and when we extend the layout on to another board, we will worry about the actual destination then.

The other point peculiar to the CNW operation is that all trains are made up of bi-level (double-deck) cars and are push-pull operated using F7 or E8 diesel locomotives. So there is no need for the locomotive to run around the train at Warren. On the actual CNW commuter routes there may be anything from two to six passenger cars, the outer one a driving unit, depending on the density of the route. A single car is not usual, but may be seen on late or holiday workings on some routes. For the compact Warren branch we decided that a single trailer would be used for early and late trains running to Chrystal Lake only and two trailers would be used for trains running 'through' to Chicago. This is actually a happy assumption. As Chrystal Lake is on the Harvard-Chicago route, itself a main line, with a very frequent commuter train service, we reasoned that trains coming off the Warren branch would not be likely to duplicate runs to Chicago on an already busy main line. So we make only the most important trains run 'through' to Chicago and for the rest the passengers boarding at Warren and Beresford change at Chrystal Lake to a train already running on the Harvard-Chicago route.

Having placed all the key passenger train times at what is roughly the correct timing by real CNW standards, we could then pencil in all the freight train timings on the branch. It is most unlikely there would ever be 'through' freight workings on a small branch like this. So we assume that all freight cars for on-line customers or facilities are dropped or picked-up overnight by main line freight trains at the Chrystal Lake interchange sidings, then brought up the branch by a small locomotive assigned to the branch. In practice this is a Minitrix Fairbanks-Morse H-12-44 or an Atlas GP9.

It so happens that the timings we have invented dove-tail quite neatly with the passenger trains, but the assumption must be made from the timings that some of the freight trains must go into passing loops or sidings down the branch to let passenger trains through. We also ignored for the present that somewhere along the 18 miles of track between Warren and Chrystal Lake there may be other on-line industries with traffic to

exchange and so make further complications. At present, therefore, all the freight cars which arrive at Warren are for sidings 'on the board', not off it.

Of particular interest is the complication with the 9.45 am local freight. Long before it can finish its work at Warren and North Warren, the 10.18 am passenger train is due. So the freight locomotive has to clear the station tracks and in practice it goes round to North Warren and the train crew take a coffee break until the passenger train has departed again as the 10.35 am.

Following the American style, we have given each train working a number, odd numbers out from Chicago and Chrystal Lake, even numbers inbound. The prefix '9' is supposed to indicate the line or branch—in this case the Warren branch. Actually this reference number is much easier to follow and remember than the time of the train and in practice the number is used rather than the time. Thus the 9.45 am referred to above is called Train No 911 when we are operating. A full weekday schedule has no less than 34 workings—17 in each direction, and it takes a very full evening operating session to get through it all. Sometimes, in fact, we do not complete it, but the beauty of the system is that you can start and stop when and how you please. If you have only a spare half hour, run as many trains as you have time for, mark your progress on the timetable (tick off each working with a pencil when completed) and carry on from where you left off when you next get time for an operating session. In CNW parlance the push-pull commuter trains are known as 'Scoots' (because they scoot along

Track plan of the Warren, Beresford and Chicago N-gauge layout built by Chris Ellis. **1** *Beresford Station;* **2** *Oil depot;* **3** *Dairy;* **4** *Corn and feed elevator;* **5** *Farm machinery and produce merchant;* **6** *Mine;* **7** *Freight depot;* **8** *Warehouse;* **9** *Warren Station;* **10** *North Warren;* **A** *fiddle siding. Each square measures 12 in. (Courtesy Chris Ellis.)*

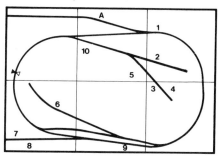

Compiling a simple timetable

quite fast!), and to save time on the timetable we have marked all passenger trains as 'scoots'. The working timetable reproduced here should be self-explanatory.

Do not be put off in any way by the fact that the trains and timetable on our actual layout are modern Chicago and North Western Railroad. You can run any trains that take your fancy on this type of layout without fundamentally changing the timetable. You can, of course, work out your own running sequence and times to suit yourself, but if you do not want to be bothered with this just photocopy our printed working timetable, change the station names and trains to suit your particular interest and away you go! With appropriate adaptations the line could be set in Wales, Scotland or Germany, the basic principles of the operation remain the same.

The other important point is that the layout and setting can equally well be in the steam or diesel age as you wish. Though our CNW 'scoots' are push-pull, there is no reason why the passenger trains should not be perfectly conventional with the locomotive running around the train for the return journey. We have done this ourselves by switching the diesel era of our layout over to steam on occasions, using the Minitrix Pennsylvania Railroad B6 0-6-0 and an 0-4-0 saddle tank. In this case the passenger train has been made up of a single 'steam age' PRR combine coach.

What we hope our timetable has shown is that even a very simple layout like this, little more than a development from a basic train set oval, still has massive operational potential far removed from merely running model trains round and round in circles. We found that when trying to work a full week-day timetable in an evening session there was not actually much time available for running trains round

and round but, if you want to make a few laps to simulate 'mileage' before bringing the train into the station, that is entirely up to you.

The above description by Chris Ellis clearly demonstrates that a simple sequence scheme of operation can create interesting and entertaining running on even a very small and simple layout, extending the enjoyment such a layout can give well beyond the period of construction. Such sequence operation is ideal for the beginner, new to the concept of model railway operation and still gaining skill in actually carrying out the various train movements. Indeed, many modellers find that the system suits them well and they continue to use it on their layouts without going on to anything more complicated. However, others feel that much of the interest, even excitement, in model railway operation comes from meeting the challenge of running to time, just as the real railways strive to do. It can be argued that as we have no real passengers on our model trains, and there is nobody sending out or waiting to receive the goods we pretend to be transporting on our railway, then we have no pressure to provide an efficient service unless we run to time. The protagonists of this argument feel that this is the best way to duplicate the operation of the real railways on a model layout. Certainly such operation can be an absorbing activity.

When introducing an operating system on a layout it is best to begin as a sequence scheme without the pressure of working to the clock. Later, as the operators become familiar with the system and gain experience generally, working to time can be added to the operating method. Basic to any system of operating to the clock is the matter of time and how we apply it to the model railway, and I would like to consider this subject next.

Time and the speeded-up clock

Now it can be argued that time is a constant factor and applies equally to models as to the real railway. And, indeed, if our model train is travelling at 60 scale miles per hour it will proceed a distance of 1 scale mile in 1 actual minute, just as the prototype at 60 miles per hour will travel 1 mile in the same actual time. So we could deduce that this is a logical argument and that we should run our timetable in accordance with an ordinary clock, and there are some modellers who do just that.

However, when we look a little further into the subject we find that there are definite disadvantages to this method. One very significant problem arises because of the short time it takes a train to run from one station to the next. Because it is usually quite impossible to model even a short branch line exactly to scale in the space we have for a layout, considerable compression is unavoidable in the model. This is selective, affecting particularly the length of track between stations. Thus, on most model railways the time taken for a train to travel between stations can be measured in seconds rather than minutes. Timetables both for the prototype and for model railways are made out to minutes, not seconds, so that these times between stations would have to be rounded up or down to the nearest minute and it is not possible to construct a satisfactory timetable on this basis. For example, if we have three stations, A, B and C on an 00-scale layout, with 10 feet of track from A to B and 20 feet from B to C, a train travelling at 20 scale miles per hour will take just under 30 seconds to go from A to B, which we must count as 0 minutes or 1 minute for our timetable. The time B to C will be just under 60 seconds, again counted as either 0 or 1 minute for the schedule. If the train travels at 40 scale miles per hour the times will be halved but must again be taken as either 0 or 1 minute for the timetable. Thus the use of standard time is quite inadequate for our purposes. If, however, we use fast time with a 12:1 ratio (5 minutes actual time becomes 1 hour fast time) the times A to B will become approximately 6 minutes

and 3 minutes respectively for 20 and 40 scale miles per hour, and similarly the times B to C will be about 12 minutes and 6 minutes. These enable us to compile a meaningful timetable.

There are many prototype operations that are unnecessarily long and it would be uninteresting on the model to allow the actual time they require. Another advantage of speeded-up time is that these functions will now take much less time. The use of fast time also makes it convenient to make small alterations in the schedules as found necessary by experience in running the layout. Say we have allowed 90 seconds for our train to pass between two points on the layout. If we use actual time this will be represented as either 1 or 2 minutes on the schedule. However, with 12:1 ratio speeded-up time this will be 18 minutes and, if necessary, we can adjust this to say 17 or 19 minutes, whereas with standard time we would still have to list it as 1 or 2 minutes.

Another reason for using speeded-up time is to retain the character of the operation of the real railways. To take an example, we can consider the intervals between trains, one following the other. On the prototype there may be an interval of 5 or 10 minutes and any delay of the first train will immediately affect the running of the second. On a model railway with an interval of 5 or 10 actual minutes the first train would have reached its destination long before the second train started, and the situation is not really representative of the operation on the prototype. With speeded-up time the actual interval on the model will be much less and the situation will be more like that on the real railway.

With many prototype timetables there are gaps in the schedule when there is no activity and these times can be boring interruptions to an operating session for which standard time is used. However, if we employ a speeded-up clock, these gaps will be very much shortened and will not be a significant interruption to the flow of operations.

Another benefit of the fast clock is that a full

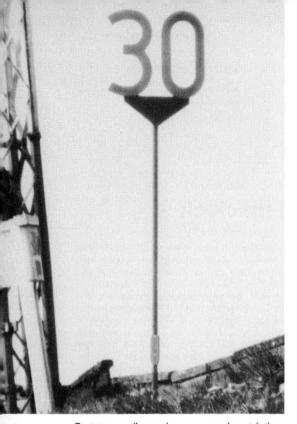

Prototype railways impose speed restrictions which must be obeyed by drivers. This is a standard British Rail speed restriction sign, the numbers indicating the limit, here 30 miles per hour. The front faces of the numbers are yellow, the rest black.

24-hour timetable can be worked through in a single operating session. This means that the whole range of railway activity, day and night, can be enjoyed giving variety and hence extra interest to the session. It also has the advantage that, by working through the complete timetable at each session, the operators become familiar with it and, as they gain experience and skill, the running of the layout will be smoother and more enjoyable.

Having put forward a case for the use of fast time in model railway operation we must now consider just how fast this time should be. Some modellers assume that the ratio of fast to real time should relate to the scale in which they are working in some mathematically calculable way, but this is not so. A fundamental principal of the use of fast time in model railway operation is that there is no 'correct' scale time ratio for a particular scale; the ratio depends only on operating considerations. At first sight this may seem illogical but if we consider the situation in more detail we can see that it is not basically the scaling down that introduces the need for fast time. As mentioned in an example earlier, a model train will travel a scale mile at, say, 60 scale miles per hour in the same actual time, 1 minute, as a real train will take for a mile at 60 miles per hour. So, purely on the basis of scaling down, there is not necessarily any reason why we should not use standard time. It is the further compression of distances along the track, beyond that called for by scale, needed to fit a layout into a reasonable space that is a fundamental reason for using speeded-up time. We also find that many manoeuvres can be carried out more quickly on a model railway than on the prototype and this is a further reason for employing fast time.

This speeded-up time is often known as 'fast time'. Sometimes the term 'scale time' is used but, as this may be thought to imply some relationship to the scale of the model, it is perhaps not as good a term as 'fast time'. There have been attempts to justify the use of a particular relationship of this fast time to scale using various mathematical principles. For example, it has been suggested that we should apply Froude's equation, which is used to relate findings from the testing of models in wind tunnels and water tanks to the prototypes. Or that we should use the equation employed by movie makers when filming models to determine the appropriate camera speed so that, when screened at normal projection speed, the models in the film will move, and particularly fall, like the real thing. However, the idea of applying these principles to model railway operation is fallacious because, as explained above, the ratio depends not on the scale of the layout but on various operating considerations, though as it happens the results obtained do come within the range used by railway modellers.

Factors which do influence your choice include the distance between stations, train speeds and the efficiency of the operators at shunting and in carrying out other train movements of this type. It is also useful to choose a ratio which is convenient for measurementrs and calculations; the minimum interval of time should be a fast minute as we do not want to be involved with fractions of minutes in our schedule. The length of the 'day' on your railway, which may be 12 or 24 hours or some other period, and the average time you like an operating session to last may also influence your choice as there are advantages in being able to work through a full 'day' at a single session.

The ideal ratio depends to some extent on the type of operation on your railway. If it is

Operating your trains at scale speeds will improve the realism of your layout and you can impose appropriate scale speed limits. Suitable model signs are available from Smiths of Solihull and from R. Alderman of Yeovil. The mm example shown here is from a Smiths set.

Mainly running trains out on the line then, because of our greatly compressed distances, considerable speeding up of the time is desirable, especially if our stations are close together. On the other hand, if operation on our layout is largely shunting, perhaps on an industrial railway model, then the ratio should be smaller. One argument put forward against the use of fast time is that the discrepancy between the two types of operation will make it impossible to select a suitable ratio. These modellers claim that as shunting on the model will take much the same time as on the prototype, then using a speeded-up clock to make main line running more realistic will leave insufficient time for shunting to be carried out properly, or that inordinately long times will be needed on the timetable for shunting operations to be completed. In fact, two American modellers carefully timed shunting activities of various types on both prototypes and model railroads and found that, though it varies between different types of shunting, on

average such operations were still appreciably faster on the model. They were, incidentally, very careful that all model locomotive movements were carried out at scale speeds and in accordance with prototype practice. It is, therefore, quite feasible to find a compromise ratio which will improve operation on the main line and still permit realistic shunting.

The usual range of ratios of fast to standard time is somewhere between 6:1 and 15:1, with 12:1 perhaps the most popular, though 10:1 also has its advocates. The 12:1 ratio is convenient in that 5 minutes of standard time is equivalent to 1 hour of fast time, and a 24-hour day on the timetable can be worked through in a 2-hour operating session. The choice of ratio is up to the individual modeller and there is no reason why he should not adjust it later if he finds that it is set too high or too low for his layout. It has been suggested that a variable speed clock, or 'rubber' clock, is advantageous with inexperienced operators. If they fall behind schedule or are having difficulties of one sort or another then the clock can be slowed, or even stopped, until they catch up or sort out the problems. This has benefits when learning, both for training the operators and in deciding which will be the best ratio for your layout. However, once the operators have sufficient experience and the appropriate ratio has been selected it is best to try to stick to the proper timing and not to alter the clock. With

Time and the speeded-up clock

practice in working at a particular ratio, the operators become used to the fast time and familiar with the time needed for various manoeuvres and this is valuable in running the layout well. If the clock is being continually varied it takes much longer for this skill to be acquired.

Obviously, the most convenient method of working to fast time is to have a clock, or clocks, which have been adapted or altered in some way so that fast time can be read directly from it. Various modellers have modified clocks in different ways, usually by altering the gearing, so that they run faster. The details will vary with the particular clocks and with the degree of speeding-up required, and such alterations are beyond the scope of this book. I understand that digital clocks with integrated circuits can be altered by replacing the original time-base oscillator with one of higher frequency, or even with a variable frequency to produce a variable clock. Two articles have appeared in the American magazine, *Model Railroader,* one on altering an electric kitchen clock in the November 1955 issue, and one on modifying a digital clock in the November 1974 issue, and modellers wanting further information may like to refer to these articles.

A much simpler method is to use a clock without altering the mechanism but removing the hour hand and using the minute hand to read off the hours on a new face made up to suit the ratio selection. If you choose 12:1 you do not even need to make a new face, merely read off the hours as usual but with the minute hand. You can judge the intermediate times fairly well, especially if the spaces are marked out into minutes on the dial. If you are making a new clock face yourself you can divide the spaces between the hour marks into four quarters, each representing 15 minutes of fast time. Obviously reading a clock of this type will not be quite as accurate as one with the mechanism altered to speed it up but the times can still be judged sufficiently accurately for satisfactory operation.

To conclude our consideration of speeded-up time there is one final concept, that of the shortened mile, named the 'smile' by its originator, the late Frank Ellison, a pioneer of realistic model railroad operation. This measure is not related to scale but to the fast time ratio. A model train travelling at 60 scale miles per hour goes 1 scale mile in 1 minute of standard time; it also goes 1 'smile' in 1 fast minute. Thus the length of a 'smile' depends on the fast time ratio employed; for 10:1, for example, 1 'smile' = 0.1 scale mile. Though some modellers do install 'smile' posts at appropriate spacing on their main lines, 'smiles' do not really apply visually or in construction, but relate to timetable operation.

The train graph

Earlier we looked at a very simple timetable for a branch line with only one engine in steam. Here scheduling is very simple as there is only one train to be concerned with at any one time, running from the fiddle yard to the terminus and back. Because of the simplicity of the train movements, a mere list or table of the times is easy to compile and to interpret. On a more complex layout with perhaps two or three trains making journeys at the same time, and the need to arrange for trains to pass at specific places where there are passing loops, then a table of that type is much more difficult to compile and to understand. We need some other method which will enable us to determine more easily and quickly the relative positions and movements of the trains.

The simplest method is to follow the example of the prototype railways and make up a train graph on which the information is built up in an easy to understand visual form. It enables us to see, at a glance, where any train should be at any time and where and when it will pass other trains. These graphs, by convention, are laid out with the distance on the vertical axis. For the modeller this can be in scale miles, in actual feet, or if using fast time, in 'smiles'. It is useful to include a schematic track diagram along this axis also, together with the station names appropriately positioned. This is set out along the horizontal axis of the graph, either actual time or fast time, depending on the system you use on your layout. On such a graph the slope of the train lines is related to their speeds. When a train is stopped the train line will be horizontal, that is, though time passes, the distance does not change. The operators can work from train graphs or timetables can be compiled from the graph for running purposes. If you plan to work from the train graph it is convenient to make photocopies of the original graph for the

Each division is a short mile ('smile)

An example of a train graph.

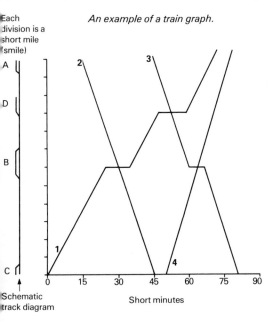

Schematic track diagram

Short minutes

If vertical axis scale miles instead of 'smiles', plot real time along horizontal axis instead of short minutes (fast time). Goods Train **1** leaves Station C at 0 minutes and stops at Station B at 25 minutes to shunt and to allow Train **2**, a non-stopping passenger train, to pass. Train **1** also waits on Siding D to allow Train **3** to pass. Train **2** reaches Station C and is turned to become Train **4** leaving 5 minutes later. Train **3** is a goods train which stops at Station B to shunt and to allow Train **4** to pass.

Average speed of a train is given by the slope.

Train 2 travels 12 smiles from A to C in 30 fast minutes — average speed thus 24 miles per hour.

The train graph

Above *Once we have established our standard timetable we can increase the operating activity by adding extra unscheduled trains. An interesting example is an enthusiast's special which will give us the opportunity to run a locomotive and stock which might otherwise be inappropriate to the line. This scene was specially set up on the Isle of Purbeck MRC's 00-gauge Swanage branch layout with a Triang 'Lord of the Isles' heading the train.* **Below** *Another instance where a special unscheduled train can add to the interest of timetable operation. This is the snowplough train, rather rarely required in Britain, but regularly needed on many European and American lines in the winter. This train is on a Swiss narrow-gauge line.*

operators to use, and these can be marked to show the features of importance to the particular operator. For example, if one operator is concerned with running an intermediate junction station on the line, a red line can be drawn horizontally across the graph at the level of the station. It is then easy for that operator to see exactly when the various trains reach his station as this will be where the train lines cut the red line. Alternatively, if one operator will be running certain trains then on his copy of the train graph his trains can have their lines marked in red. The train graphs represent a point to point system but can also be applied to an oval layout perfectly satisfactorily. In this case one point on the oval (perhaps one station or yard, or, best of all, if there are hidden sidings at one side of the oval serving as a fiddle yard) is included at both the top and the bottom of the vertical axis of the graph. To avoid confusion it can be named differently for the two positions. Once a train has arrived at this point it can either reverse forming a train returning from this yard or it can go on when it will be a new train starting at the other end of the axis on the train graph.

Ideally, the train graph is constructed, as mentioned above, with distance plotted on the vertical axis, positioning stations and other points accurately on this axis according to their situation on the layout, measuring in scale miles, actual feet or 'smiles'. We can then plot the train lines exactly either working from the times we want the trains to be at particular points, or on the basis of the speed, because the slope of the train lines relates to the speed—the faster the train the more nearly vertical the train line. Thus working from the time the train leaves a station we can determine by drawing in the appropriate slope when it will reach the next station travelling at the speed we have chosen. This may, for example, be 60 scale miles per hour for a passenger train, and only 20 miles per hour for a slow goods train.

However, if we want to keep things simple and do not wish to measure the distances on the layout, or calculate them in terms of scale miles, it is still possible to construct a train graph by working more empirically. To do this we run the various trains we intend to include in the timetable over the layout. Taking care to run them at what appear to the eye to be suitable scale speeds, each journey is carefully timed for each point on the trip and these are noted down. We then construct a train graph as before but, instead of plotting distances on the vertical axis, we merely list the stations on the route in their correct order along this axis. They can either be spaced evenly regardless of their actual distances apart or they can be placed approximately as they are located in relation to each other on the layout. Such a graph will not yield all the information that the more accurately plotted one will; we cannot, for example, calculate the train speed from the slope of the train line. However, the graph can still be a very useful method of constructing a suitable timetable for operating the layout and a helpful visual presentation of that timetable for the operators.

So far both in simple timetable construction and in the train graph we have been concerned only with the scheduled trains which are run regularly on the layout. After a time when the timetable becomes very familiar and perhaps a little repetitious, some enthusiasts like to add a little extra challenge and interest to the proceedings by introducing unscheduled extra trains and other complications. The need to cope with these, while at the same time interfering as little as possible with the regular trains on the timetable will certainly stop the operators getting bored! One method of introducing these complications at random, thus making the session more exciting, is to have a set of cards, sometimes called situation or hazard cards, on each of which is listed a situation which will affect operation. These can include changes in the traffic needs necessitating the running of an extra train or of providing additional coaches for one which is already scheduled, breakdowns or derailments which may entail delays or diversions as well as the making up of a breakdown train and running it to the location, and so on. The list of possibilities is almost limitless and you can easily select some which are appropriate to your layout. The cards are shuffled and the pack is placed face down. Then, at predetermined times during an operating session, a card can be taken from the top of the pack and the instructions carried out. The introduction of unscheduled events at random in this way can do a great deal to add interest and challenge to a session, even if the basic timetable is becoming rather routine.

The train graph

Bell codes

On the prototype railway bell signals sent from one signal box to the next advise the signalmen of the trains passing into the areas which they control. The messages are passed in a code system with which the signalmen are as familiar as a radio operator is with the morse code. Rather than merely exchanging information by direct conversation, some railway modellers like to use the standard British Rail bell signalling codes for communication between two or more operators running a model railway layout. The system is not only convenient, particularly if the layout is a large one with the operators some distance apart, perhaps even in different rooms, but is also authentic, adding realism to operating procedures.

The prototype codes are designed to cover every possible contingency, and are further complicated by the fact that some codes apply to all British Rail regions, some to all regions

Below Part of the fiddle yard on Eric Kay's N-gauge Sherrington branch. The fiddle yard operator uses the gong at the right to communicate by bell code with the other operator at the station. Note the check list showing the codes commonly used on the layout. **Below right** *Simple bell code system as used on the Sherrington Branch.*

except the Southern, and some to the Southern Region only! For the full details I would refer you to the very useful book, *British Railway Signalling* by G.M. Kichenside and Alan Williams, published by Ian Allan, where the BR Standard Signal Box Bell Codes are given in full in an appendix. Most modellers find that a restricted code is adequate for their needs and is much easier to learn, so that operators quickly find they no longer have to keep referring back to the list. As an example, the bell code presented here is the one that Eric Kay used on his Sherrington Branch and which proved perfectly adequate for normal operation, both at home and at exhibitions. When there were two operators on his layout, one would man the terminus station, Sherrington, and the other the fiddle yard and the bell code was employed for communication between them to offer and accept trains.

I would advise the beginner who would like to use the bell code system to start with a simple selection, rather than with too full a list which will be difficult to use. It is easy to add further codes as necessary later. The actual bells can be merely bell gongs, struck by hand, or an electric bell system can be installed, arranged so that each press of a button or switch gives a single ring.

Opening signal box	5-5-5
Closing signal box	7-5-5
Call Attention	1
Is line clear for:	
Express passenger train	4
Ordinary passenger train	3-1
Branch auto-train	1-3
Empty coaching stock	2-2-1
Light Engine	2-3
Train entering section	2
Branch goods train	1-2

Card order systems

looking at operation on a model railway
layout, so far we have concentrated on the
movement of complete trains, passenger and
freight, over the line in accordance with a
schedule. We have considered how to compile
a timetable based on a realistic pattern of
operation to handle the traffic appropriate to
the line. As yet we have not taken into account
the distribution of individual goods wagons,
vans and other stock. On a branch line we have
merely sent a goods train made up from what
appears to be a reasonable selection of stock
from the fiddle yard to the terminus. At this
destination we have perhaps exchanged the
incoming wagons for ones already at the
station and which are assumed to be ready to
go back to the junction (fiddle yard).

While recognising that it is desirable for
realism that our goods stock should appear to
be moving in response to the traffic needs, we
have no automatic method of producing an
authentic traffic flow and must either improvise
as we go or have a set scheme laid down for
our sequence operation or timetable. Neither
system is ideal. The former tends to lead to any
wagons which are not easy to get at, being
ignored when shunting is carried out, while the
latter is likely to become too well known to the
operator in time, making operation too
predictable and, therefore, less interesting. On
the prototype railways the needs of the
customers dictate the traffic and, as these
needs fluctuate, so the goods traffic varies, but
we have no customers on our model railway.

In an effort to create, artificially, realistic and
varying goods traffic in model railway operation, a number of systems of freight car distribution have been devised. I use the American
term 'freight car' deliberately because there
has been a particular interest in this subject in
the United States and most of the schemes
have originated there. The systems have been
designed to represent American prototype
railroad practice, particularly the operations of
the 'way freight' train which travels the single
track main line stopping to drop and pick up
cars at numerous stations and lineside

industries. However, the schemes can also be
applied with good effect on British layouts with
only minor adaptations. Freight car distribution
systems are ideal for small shunting layouts
such as those based on industrial railways and
can create very interesting operation on a small
layout. On other lines, for example a country
branch, the systems can be used in
combination with a timetable, and will provide
the basis for the distribution of goods stock to
and from the terminus and any intermediate
stations or lineside industries by the trains
listed in the schedule.

In one of the simplest forms of random
distribution selection, modellers have used
playing cards, deciding beforehand which card
or cards from the pack will represent which
destination for the rolling stock. When the train
is ready to depart the cards are shuffled and
dealt from the top of the pack. The first card
shows where the first wagon is to go, the
second card the second wagon, and so on. As
all destinations will not be appropriate for all
wagons it will be necessary on occasions to
ignore the card turned up for a particular
wagon and to turn up others until a suitable
one is found.

A variant which will overcome the problem
of unsuitable destinations is to have groups of
destinations, each of which can accept any
wagon. For example, one group could be made
up of several industrial sidings. If a wagon is
directed here it can be shunted onto a siding
which is appropriate for use. Another group
may be a goods yard with various facilities;
thus a cattle wagon directed to the goods
yard would be put on the siding serving the
cattle dock. If we have four groups we can, as
suggested by Mr Evens in *Model Railways*
magazine (January 1974) use a pack of cards
with the court cards removed and use the
categories of cards red-even, red-odd, black-
even, and black-odd, to give the four groups.

The true card order systems, however, do
not rely on playing cards but have cards, one for
each wagon on the railway, on which enough
information to identify each individual wagon,

Card order systems

```
OWNER:      HIGHLEY MINING COMPANY.
TYPE:       10 TON OPEN WAGON.
NO.         425.

DESTINATION:

Colliery.

Coal Staithes.

Smiths Factory.

Crowley Manufacturing Company.

Johnson's Foundry.

Fiddle Yard.
```

*A wagon card for a simp.
card order system. A pape
clip is used as a marker i
indicate destination on left*

van, tanker, etc, is provided. There are many ways in which distribution of the rolling stock can then be organised. One simple system is to have another set of cards with all possible destinations, again one card for each. The two sets of cards are shuffled separately and the top card from each is turned up providing a wagon and its destination. This process is then repeated as many times as there are to be wagons in the train. Again there may be the problem of inappropriate destinations turning up with the need to go on to another card. A similar system could be employed to determine which wagons the train picks up, or alternatively, one wagon could be collected for each one dropped.

Another scheme is to include on each wagon card a note of the appropriate load and the origin and destination for that load. The cards belonging to the wagons which are at a particular station are kept in a small box at the station. When a train arrives the driver takes a number of cards from the box, collects the wagons concerned, and takes them, and their cards, to the appropriate destinations; if a wagon begins at its destination then it is returned to its origin as an empty. The number of cards taken can be at the driver's discretion, or previously decided, or determined at the time by throwing a dice. This system in its simplest form will mean that any particular wagon will only move between two places, origin to destination and back. A more interesting variant is to have all the possible destinations for a particular wagon listed across the top or along one side of the card and to select one of these, indicating which with a paper clip, before the run.

There are many variants of the card order system but I would like to describe one simple system which can be applied to a small layout and which you may find suitable for your

model railway. If you do employ it you shoul find it a useful basis, though as you gai experience you will probably wish to mak modifications to suit the particular features your line.

Strictly, card order systems should apply loads and allow for whether or not a wago van, etc is empty or loaded, but if we concer ourselves only with rolling stock movemen we can simplify the system to advantage. Th method can be applied to a fiddle yard terminus layout, to a through station type layout with a fiddle yard at each end, or to a oval continuous scheme. Obviously the mor stations, sidings and industries that we ca include on the layout, the greater will be th scope for stock distribution and the mor entertaining the operation.

The initial step is to list all the possib destinations including goods sidings of variou types at different stations and any industries these stations or along the line. A card (a plai postcard is suitable) is made out for each iter of goods rolling stock on the railway indicatir its type, number and, in the case of Privat Owner stock, the name of the owner, to hel easy identification during operation. Below th list the possible destinations. If you have a la out with one or more through stations and yard or fiddle yard at each end, or a continuou layout with part concealed and used as a fidd yard for trains coming either way round th oval, you can also include TGA and TGB regular intervals in the listings, standing fc 'Through Goods' with the 'A' or 'B' indicatin the direction of travel along or around th track. In this case the wagon will be take through to the yard at the other end of th journey and will wait there until another train made up. At each station, yard or industrial sit there will be a box for cards, divided into a arrivals side and a departures side. If there a everal sidings at that point the two sides will ach be subdivided into sections for each iding. These boxes can easily be made from tout card with thinner card for the subdividing ieces.

When we start an operating session the tock will normally be spread around the layout n various sidings and the card for each wagon /ill be in the box at the site at which the wagon s located. We can make up a train in the yard r fiddle yard by taking the required number of ards from the box there and then assembling ne wagons concerned in the yard. On each ard there will be a paper clip marking one of ne destinations and the operator distributes ne stock from the train into the indicated idings as the train makes its journey along the ne. On arrival at a siding for which his train as a wagon the driver looks in the box. If there s a card, or cards, in the departures section he emoves this and then transfers any card in the rrivals section into the departures side. The ard or cards for any wagons to be dropped at ne siding he places in the arrivals side. After arrying out the necessary shunting to drop nd pick up wagons as required, the driver akes his train on, together with the remaining ards from his original selection, plus the cards or any wagons he has picked up here. On the ards he picks up he moves the paper clips own to the next destination on the list. If it is n his route he can drop these wagons, if not e takes them through to the yard at the end of ne journey where they will wait for a train in ne other direction.

In fact there are quite a number of variations ossible regarding picking up wagons. One requently used is to only pick up wagons that re to travel in the direction of the train; others re left for the first train in the opposite irection. Some modellers like to pick up the ame number of wagons at a siding as are ropped there; this has the advantage of alancing the stock around the layout auto- atically. Although on this system each /agon runs through the same pattern of distri- ution repeatedly, the clip being moved back o the top of the list when it reaches the ottom, the number of destinations on the

cards will vary from wagon to wagon so there will be almost limitless variation in the way trains are made up, especially if there are a reasonable number of wagons and destinations. Variety can also be added by listing destinations in differing orders on the various cards.

Though this system is a fairly simple one I think you will find that it gives a sense of purpose to the running of goods trains on your layout. No longer are you just picking up a few wagons here and there as the mood takes you, and for no particular reason; instead you are moving wagons following the instructions given providing a fair representation of the real railway, responding to the needs of its customers.

One of the main criticisms of the card order systems is the need for the cards to be carried by the driver from place to place with the train, and the difficulty of marrying up a wagon with its card again if the two become separated. In fact these problems only really apply on large layouts with numerous wagons and with considerable actual distances between different parts of the layout. On a small layout a simple card order system, as described above, should be perfectly satisfactory. On some lay- outs, in an attempt to overcome the problems just mentioned, systems have been devised where the freight car itself carries either a slip of paper or a drawing pin, the head of which is coloured according to a code, which tells the operator where it is to go.

Cliff Young, a modeller living in Britain but modelling American prototype, uses a card and waybill system for freight operation based on one devised by an American modeller, Doug Smith, but modified to suit his own require- ments. The system is more complicated than the simple one I described above but corres- pondingly is more flexible and realistic. He has given details of his system in an article in the November 1966 issue of *Railway Modeller* magazine and also in the recently published book *The Encyclopaedia of Model Railways* from Octopus Books Ltd, and I would recommend that readers interested in taking the subject further should consult his articles.

Card order systems

Loading and unloading

As we have already seen, for realism in the operation of a model railway layout we must give the impression that it is actually transporting people and goods from place to place, reproducing in miniature the function of the prototype. However, because our miniature railway workers cannot load and unload our wagons and vans for us, we do run into problems with appearances in this respect. So often on model railways we see a train arrive and shunt a wagon loaded with coal on to a siding, only to have the wagon taken away again by the next train still full of coal! With much of our rolling stock there is, of course, no difficulty. Though a few modellers do include passengers inside model coaches, it is not generally very noticeable whether coaches are full or empty so we can consider them as whichever we need according to the requirements of our timetable. And there is obviously nothing we can do to simulate passengers getting on and off the trains! Similarly with goods stock such as vans, tankers, cement wagons, salt wagons, and so on, the loaded and empty stock appears identical. If we wish to preserve the correct procedures we can shunt vans into a goods shed or under a canopy outside the door of a warehouse, tankers can be positioned alongside storage tanks, cement wagons beneath a hopper, and so on, where we can imagine loading or unloading is taking place without distorting realism too much.

The difficulty comes with open wagons,

timber bolsters, flat wagons, and suchlike Some modellers just load and unload openly b hand, ignoring appearances for the short tim taken. If you are exhibiting your layout yo may prefer to arrange things so this procedur takes place out of sight of the public. On possibility is to run the stock into a goods shed warehouse or factory building which has n back so that you have access to the interior fc loading and unloading without viewers bein aware of this. Alternatively you may be able t run the stock on to a hidden siding or to th fiddle yard. Whatever you do, the process c loading and unloading is made much easie with specially made loads. For an open wagor cut a rectangle of balsa or thick card to f neatly into the top of the wagon. On top of thi glue the coal, rock chippings, sand, barrels sacks, boxes, or whatever other load you wis to represent. On the underside glue a sma block of wood, of the right size to support th load at the correct level inside the wagon, a the centre. This arrangement makes it easy t remove the load; merely pressing on one en will cause it to tilt so that you can pick it up Replacing the load is also easy and, of course the loads can be used for different wagon provided the dimensions are the same.

A system which can be very realistic if w are modelling trains transporting bulk load between two places, for example, ore bein taken from a mine to a processing plant, is t have two trains which are identical, except fc the fact that one has full wagons and the othe empty wagons. With the arrangement of th tracks it appears that loaded trains are emergir from the mine and running into the processir plant, while the reverse is taking place with th empty trains.

There are also a number of working mode loaders of various types now available as kits c ready-to-use models and, with these, wagor can actually be loaded and unloaded adding the realism of operation. An example is th Faller Gravel Works complete with storag silos, working conveyor belts and operatir hopper wagons.

Removable wagon load with narrow central support beneath false floor. Pressing at one end tilts load for easy removal.

Above *The marshalling sidings of the hump shunting yard at the Tyne Yard. Though, obviously, considerable simplification and compression is necessary, an interesting and realistic hump yard can be included on a large or moderate sized model railway layout.* **Below** *A van passing through a retarder on the Tyne Yard hump yard.*

Loading and unloading

Two views of an operating model hump yard on a large HO-scale Fleischmann exhibition layout. **Top** The hump itself is in the centre of this picture. **Above** The five marshalling sidings of the hump yard are shown in the right centre of this photograph. On this automatically operated layout, wagons are distributed at random on to these sidings. **Below** Part of the track plan of the HO-scale Fleischmann exhibition layout. The small black triangle near the left side indicates the site of the hump, the lap point (three-way) is labelled 227, and the five tracks of the marshalling yard are in the central part of the diagram. (Courtesy of Fleischmann.)

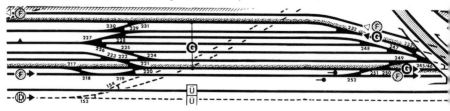

One of the most interesting aspects of the handling of freight traffic on modern prototype railways is the marshalling of wagons and vans in hump yards. Models of these yards are not often seen though the Reverend Edward Beal built one for his well-known West Midland layout nearly 30 years ago! Real hump yards occupy a great deal of space but considerable compression is possible for a model and, while one could not be included on a small layout, it would be possible to fit one in on a moderate sized home or club layout if desired. The accompanying photographs show an HO-scale working hump yard, automatically operated, on a large Fleischmann exhibition layout. An interesting point is that the yard was built entirely with standard Fleischmann parts. The single track passing over the hump has an uncoupler on the slope beyond the hump after which it divides into three by a lap point. The outer two tracks then divide again by ordinary turnouts giving a total of five marshalling sidings on which the trains are assembled. By means of contacts on the tracks, wagons passing along the tracks change the points for the following wagons.

Shunting competitions

With many systems the operating of a model railway layout can be considered as a form of game, with the challenge of keeping the layout running efficiently while overcoming any complications which arise or are deliberately introduced, all the time obeying the rules and trying to maintain realism. Part of the skill developed in operating relates to shunting, so that with practice the enthusiast becomes better both at planning his moves and at

actually carrying them out smoothly, realistically and efficiently. Taking this a little further some modellers have produced small shunting modules designed to be used as a form of competitive game. One of the most successful of these was devised by John Allen, who was a very well-known American modeller. Basically the track plan is a run-around loop with a selection of sidings and the aim is to distribute a number of freight cars placed on the module in accordance with a pre-set plan. There are many different ways in which the module can be used and the game has proved very popular.

Often with puzzles of this sort the number of moves taken are counted but John Allen chose instead to arrange for a constant slow locomotive speed and for the competition to be carried out against the clock. Thus it is important to be quick rather than to take the least possible number of moves. Used in its original form the module was very interesting but a further development was to build a mirror image unit and to link the two, so that two people can operate, one on each module, at the same time. Though the two could compete against each other, the game is carried out with them trying to help each other so that their time is taken as the time for both to have completed the required moves.

Shunting games of this type have great potential for entertainment and also for practice in operation. Full details of John Allen's layout were given in the November 1972 issue of *Model Railroader* magazine and anyone contemplating building such a module might like to refer to that article.

Maintenance

If the model railway layout is to provide interesting, enjoyable and realistic operation it is essential that the models should work well. Even for very simple operation poor running, frequent derailments, coupling faults and other interruptions will spoil the fun and may well cause the modeller to lose interest. Most of the ready-to-run equipment now available is of very good quality, but, for continued good running, regular maintenance is necessary. Some modellers neglect such attention because they feel it will be an uninteresting and time-consuming chore, others, particularly beginners, because they do not know how to tackle the job. Undeniably on a large and complex layout a great deal of time must be spent on cleaning, checking, adjusting and repairing and this is one of the reasons why the beginner should be careful not to attempt to build too ambitious a model railway layout. If

he does manage to complete such a model he may find that he has so much maintenance to do he has little time left to sit back and operate his railway. However, on a smaller, simple layout even the beginner should be able to carry out these important tasks quickly and easily and there is no doubt that the enjoyment and satisfaction obtained from the consequent smooth, reliable running will more than compensate for the time and effort.

Obviously prevention is always better than cure, in railway modelling as well as in medicine! Much can be done to avoid future troubles by good initial construction and by care in handling, operating and storing locomotives, rolling stock, track, structures and other items. Care of your models is very important and right from the beginning, with the train set, it is worth getting into good habits. After all the standard of many ready-to-

Below Maintenance vehicles are important on the full size railways. This SR two-car electric set is a rail cleaning and de-icing unit. **Below right** A re-railer makes the placing of rolling stock on the rails easier and is especially useful for N-gauge bogie rolling stock. Because it makes it easier to re rail stock less handling is likely to be necessary and there is therefore less risk of accidental damage. In this picture an Eggerbahn re-railer is being used to place a Peco N-gauge tank wagon on the track.

un models is now so good that you may well want to retain them for use on a scale layout. Alternatively, if you come to sell or exchange them you will get a better deal if they are in good condition and have clearly been properly looked after. With the train set, track and points can easily be broken, twisted or bent when setting up or dismantling the layout if due care is not taken. Do not hold pieces of track in mid air when fitting them together as this may lead to twisting and distortion of the pieces with consequent derailments. Instead, place the two track sections on a flat surface and slide them together. Never force together any pieces you are having difficulty with. Instead look carefully to see why they will not join up. Damage may also occur during storage between operating sessions, particularly if the models and track are just dumped into a large box, drawer or cupboard. The models can be conveniently and safely stored in their original boxes when not in use. Many manufacturers now include a pre-formed plastic packing piece into which the locomotive or item of rolling stock fits snugly within the box, and this helps to avoid damage. Alternatively, if the boxes are no longer available you can wrap the models in paper, preferably tissue paper, but newspaper will do, and pack them carefully into a box. Take special care not to damage couplings or wheels. Small detail fittings are also especially vulnerable. Pack track sections face to face in pairs in a box with the points on top. Slight, almost unnoticeable damage to or twisting of the track pieces may lead to troubles in running for which there is no apparent cause, so take the time and trouble to protect them during storage by proper packing. While considering the train set it is worth mentioning that, though you may have to lay the set out on

the floor you should not put it down on carpet if you can avoid doing so because fluff and dirt from the carpet will quickly get on to the wheels and axles and into the mechanisms.

One of the major problems for the railway modeller is the dust so often present in the atmosphere. Airborne dust and dirt are a nuisance in many ways affecting both the appearance and the performance of a model railway layout. In most rooms a deposit of dust settles over a layout in a surprisingly short time, even if the layout is in fairly regular use. It is especially noticeable on locomotives and rolling stock but soon makes the scenery and structures appear grimy also. The real thing is, of course, exposed to dirt, grime, dust and rain giving a weathered look which we try hard to duplicate to make our models realistic, but unfortunately the dust which settles on the layout does not give this effect but instead merely looks dirty!

Dust also interferes with the smooth running of our models in various ways. Dirt from the air becomes trapped in the oil or grease used to lubricate gearboxes and bearings and causes wear while dust deposits on electrical contacts and on the rails interfere with current flow making operation erratic. We can tackle the problem in two basic ways; preventing dust from reaching the railway and removing any which does. Ideally, the layout should be in an atmosphere as free of dust as possible. However, most railway modellers are only too pleased to find anywhere to put a model railway and cannot afford to be too choosy about the room where they set up their layout. Often a bedroom is the only possibility and, unfortunately, is particularly bad from this point of view as the bedclothes give rise to a lot of dust and fluff, most of which seems to find

Maintenance

its way on to the layout! Even in the lounge there is a good deal of dust from the furnishings as people move about the room, sit in the chairs, draw the curtains, and so on. The ideal is a room set aside solely for the layout, but few of us are this fortunate. If you are lucky enough to have a model railway room, plastic or lino floor tiles or covering, rather than a carpet, will reduce the amount of dust. If you want to cover in the space beneath the layout, hardboard panels are a better choice than old curtain material which is likely to harbour dust and dirt. The room should be kept as clean as possible and any sanding, filing, sawing or other work which produces dust should, if possible, be done elsewhere. Some American modellers, more accustomed to air conditioning than we are in Britain, have experimented with fans and filter-blower units in an attempt to keep dust out of the layout room but such arrangements are more elaborate and expensive than most modellers would wish to consider using.

If we cannot exclude dust from the room we can try to keep it off the layout itself. The difficulty is that most model railways are rather large compared to other types of models. It is much easier for car, ship and military modellers, for example, to put their creations into small cases or into bookcases or cabinets to keep them away from dust and dirt. Cabinets or cases of this type, preferably with glass doors, can be ideal for storing locomotives and rolling stock safely away from dust and from the risk of damage. They are easily and quickly accessible when wanted for operating and, if the doors are fitted with glass, the models can be seen by the modeller and by visitors without the need for handling. A few modellers have built small enclosed layouts, usually in the form of coffee tables with glass tops, occasionally in glass cases. An example of a small layout built into a coffee table is the 009 narrow gauge model railway constructed by Mr K.J. Churms which was illustrated in *PSL Model Railway Guides 1* and *2*. Such an arrangement creates an interesting and attractive piece of furniture and also keeps most of the dust out. However, unless the layout is very carefully sealed up, a little dust will creep in and the model will require occasional cleaning.

Covering larger layouts is less convenient but is certainly desirable unless the room is relatively dust free. The easiest and cheapest method is probably to use a sheet of clear polythene. Some form of support to hold the sheet clear of the structures, scenery and details is desirable as otherwise they are likely to be damaged by the cover as it is fitted or removed. A convenient method is to use hoops

bent up from wire and fitted on beneath the polythene. The cover will not be airtight so some dust will get under it, but it will help by keeping out most of the dust. The plastic will become dirty and should be washed from time to time. Covering and uncovering the layout for operating takes only a few minutes and is more than compensated for by the time saved in cleaning.

An even better scheme is some form of hinged lid which covers the layout when not in use but is easily raised for operation. Such an arrangement does require more work to construct and the materials needed will be more expensive. The details will depend on your layout size and shape. The Reverend Peter Denny constructed a very neat hinged cover for his Buckingham Branch layout some years ago using wood, hardboard and strawboard. His cover was counterweighted and was also fitted with lights, giving good illumination of the layout when in operation. A detailed description of the cover and its construction was given in the June 1961 issue of *Railway Modeller* magazine and I would recommend that you refer to this if you are considering making a cover of this type for your layout.

If the only place available for a model railway layout is in a room which is regularly used for other purposes such as the lounge, hall or a bedroom, an excellent arrangement is to build the layout into a piece of furniture such as a bookcase or a chest of drawers. The top can be hinged so that, when not in operation, the railway can be concealed by closing the lid, making the unit look like an ordinary piece of furniture. This system also protects the layout from accidental damage and, to a considerable extent, from dust and dirt. Ron Prattley has built a fine example of a bookcase containing an 00-gauge layout for his lounge. He made the lid removable so that it could be reversed to form an extension to the fixed part of the layout in the bookcase. The fiddle yard is a further detachable piece which fits as a drawer in the bookcase when the railway is not in use, and is illustrated in the *PSL Model Railway Guide 1: Baseboards, Track and Electrification*.

Another method sometimes employed by modellers who are short of space for a layout is to hinge the baseboard on to a wall or into a unit of furniture so that the railway can be folded down for operating and then swung up against the wall, or into the cabinet or cupboard out of the way when the running session is over. This scheme also has advantages from the point of view of keeping the layout clean as less dust will settle on it while it is standing on edge, particularly if it swings up into a unit of furniture so that there

Above *Harold Bowcott's 00-gauge layout is hinged on to the wall so that when not in use it can be stored folded up out of the way. This arrangement also helps to keep the layout clean as much less dust will settle on it in the vertical position. Shelves on the wall, arranged to fit into the operating well when the layout is folded up, provide storage for locomotives and rolling stock. Photograph by Brian Monaghan.)* **Below** *A British Rail ballast cleaner. All the railway modeller needs is a vacuum cleaner and a soft brush!*

s a covering strip above it. Harold Bowcott has constructed an 00-gauge layout which is hinged on to the wall so that it can be folded up against it, thus taking up a minimum of space when not in use. This position also keeps most of the dust off the layout.

In addition to keeping as much dust and dirt as possible away from the layout it is also important to avoid extremes of temperature, direct sunlight and damp as these can cause damage, warping, fading of the colours, and even melting of plastic structures and other items. For these reasons, sites such as lofts, where temperatures may vary greatly, cellars, garages and garden sheds, all of which may be damp, should be considered carefully before

building a layout there to make sure that conditions will be acceptable. All these locations are also inclined to be dirty and dusty unless properly finished inside.

For general cleaning of the layout a vacuum cleaner with a nozzle attachment fitted is ideal. There is no need to touch the layout with the nozzle, it can be held an inch or two above the surface thus avoiding the risk of damage. If you wish you can cover the nozzle end with wire mesh so that if any small details, such as figures, have become detached from the layout surface they will be caught by the mesh and not sucked up into the cleaner bag. A soft brush may be needed for more persistent dust, especially on structures. For locomotives and

Maintenance

Above *Eric Kay made this track cleaning wagon from an Atlas N-scale railroad car by drilling a hole in the floor to take the plastic nozzle and fixing a foam rubber pad beneath the floor. Track cleaning fluid poured into the nozzle soaks the pad and cleans the track as the car moves along the track. Lead weights fixed inside the car apply pressure on the pad.* **Below left** *This neat electric outline locomotive model is the Fleischmann N-scale track cleaning locomotive.* **Below right** *This view of the underside of the Fleischmann N-scale track cleaning locomotive clearly shows the two pads which clean the rails as the model runs on the track.*

rolling stock a small soft brush is useful for cleaning ; a convenient brush to use is one of the type sometimes employed for cleaning camera lenses and interiors in which the brush is combined with a rubber puffer so that dust in crevices can be blown out. This enables easy cleaning without risk of damage to small details. Even with fairly regular cleaning of the scenery the colours tend to become dull and dingy after a while and repainting may be necessary eventually. Lichen used for modelling bushes and trees may become brittle in time and it is then likely to crumble if touched. Its pliability can be restored by spraying it with a mixture of one part glycerine to three parts of water.

Track cleaning is especially important as it affects operation as well as appearance. Regular running of the trains does much to help keep the rails clean on their running surfaces, but most of us cannot run our trains often enough for this alone to be sufficient. In addition we will need to clean the rails with a little solvent fairly regularly to remove oil and dirt. The solvent can be methylated spirits or one of the commercially available track cleaners on the market. It can be applied with a soft piece of cloth or with a track cleaning wagon. Several manufacturers produce model wagons or vans which actually clean the track, either by means of a foam pad or by one or two rotating pads beneath the vehicle. In addition Fleischmann make a track cleaning locomotive in N gauge. Some modellers use WD 40 for

rack cleaning and this is effective but, as it is a little oily, it should be kept off the track surroundings. For more vigorous cleaning, perhaps when the layout has not been run for some time, a track cleaning rubber such as that made by Peco can be employed. Do not use abrasives such as sandpaper or emery cloth as these will leave scratches on the rails which predispose to the accumulation of more dirt with a recurrence of the problems. Points should also be carefully cleaned including the backs of the blades and stock rails to ensure good electrical contact. Make sure that there is no dirt or loose ballast preventing full movement of the point blades. Remove any fluff which is caught up on the rails and brush away any dust. Also check the frog for any build up of dirt deposits. When cleaning the track check also for any loose track pins, any loss of alignment at track joins and for loose fishplates, and carry out any repairs needed.

A recently introduced device which maintains good electrical conduction, even if the track is dirty, is the Relco High Frequency Generator. This unit uses high frequency superimposed on the normal supply to ionise the gap due to dirt on the track and restore electrical contact. The device converts the 12-volt DC input into high frequency AC only when the circuit is broken, burning away the dirt and restoring conductivity. The normal DC current then flows again. The generator is easily wired into the layout input and is perfectly safe to use.

It is also worth mentioning that the Multiple Train Control systems now on the market from Airfix and Hornby are less affected by dirty track than the conventional system because of the higher voltage employed and because it is constantly applied. On the ordinary 12-volt DC system the actual voltage applied is often much lower than 12 volts. I understand that the Relco HF Generator must not be used with the Multiple Train Control systems.

The full benefits of track cleaning will not be realised unless you also clean the wheels of your locomotives and rolling stock. Dirt collects on locomotive wheels and interferes with electrical pick-up; it can also spread from

Top right When the layout has not been operated recently the use of a track cleaning rubber such as that made by Peco is an effective way of cleaning the rails. **Above right** *A pipe cleaner with the tip dipped into methylated spirits or other track cleaner is useful for cleaning points.* **Right** *A Relco HF Generator for track cleaning.*

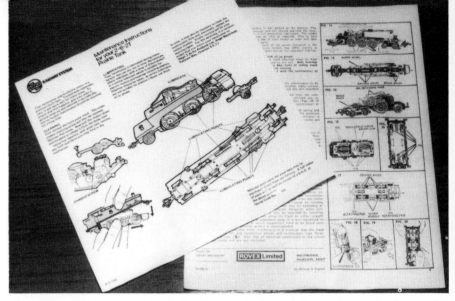

Above *The manufacturers issue instruction sheets for their locomotives and other models detailing how lubrication and maintenance should be carried out and the modeller should study the relevant information carefully. The examples shown here are from Airfix and Hornby.* **Right** *A van derailed at Gävle on the Swedish State Railway system. When any incident of this type occurs on the prototype railways a careful check is made to determine the cause. On a model railway layout we need not be so painstaking but if repeated derailments occur at the same spot or with the same piece of rolling stock then some investigation is called for.*

the wheels on to the track. For cleaning locomotive driving wheels Peco make a wheel cleaning brush and scraper set which is very effective. The wires from the brush and scraper are connected either to the 12-volt power unit terminals or to the track and, when the brush and scraper are applied to the driving wheels, one on each side, the wheels rotate making cleaning easy and effective. Sometimes scraping with a small screwdriver is necessary to remove firmly adherent dirt. On rolling stock wheels the dirt has less direct effect on running but it will spread on to the track so cleaning the rolling stock wheels is also important. Gentle scraping with a small screwdriver is the most effective method. Also look for fluff and hairs wound round axles and in bearings on both locomotives and rolling stock and remove them with a needle point and a pair of fine tweezers.

Generally locomotive mechanisms require relatively little attention and, if running well, they should, for the most part, be left well alone. Most are ready to run when purchased and do not even need oiling. In fact, many more problems arise from over oiling model locomotives than from them having insufficient lubrication. It is particularly important to avoid getting oil onto the commutator or brushes of the motor. The correct type of oil should be used; do not use thick oil or grease. Some oils can damage plastic so it is advisable to use one of the oils especially marketed for railway

modelling such as Peco Electrolube. The instruction leaflets provided by the manufacturer will indicate the lubricating points on the locomotive concerned and you should follow the advice given in these instructions. Only apply a tiny drop of oil at each point. These include the axle bearings, the coupling rod pins, valve gear pivots, and the felt oil retaining pads on the armature shaft bearing.

From time to time it may be necessary to clean the slots between the segments of the commutator as carbon from the brushes accumulates here and interferes with smooth running. To do this the brush pressure on the commutator is relieved or the brushes are removed and a wooden toothpick can then be used to remove the deposit. It is important not to scratch the surface of the commutator or the armature windings. Any oil on the commutator should be wiped off with a clean rag. If the brushes are worn they can be replaced at this time.

If you are in any doubt about your ability to carry out any of these jobs do take the model to your local dealer rather than risk causing damage. Always read the instruction leaflets carefully before doing anything to your model locomotives. Never take them apart just for the sake of it if they are running satisfactorily and never remove the magnet from the motor as it will lose its power unless it is kept in contact with a keeper all the time.

If a locomotive will not run, though it has operated satisfactorily previously, this may be due to there being no power to the track or to a fault in the locomotive or its electrical pick-up. A simple means of checking for a fault in the supply to the track is to try another locomotive on the same piece of track. If this will not run either make sure that the power is actually switched on and that there are no loose connections between the power unit and the track. Also check that the fishplates are tight and providing proper electrical contact. Never fiddle with the mains side of the power unit and never open the power unit casing, as accidents with the mains supply can be fatal. If you suspect a fault here take the unit to your local dealer for expert advice.

If the track is not at fault we need to check the locomotive. Remove the body and apply wires from the 12-volt DC output of the power unit direct to the brushes, one to each. The motor will then usually run. If so, then the current is not reaching the motor from the track and this may be due to dirty wheels, a pick-up not in contact with its wheel, or a lead which has come loose. It is usually fairly easy to spot which of these is the cause. If, when the wires are applied to the brushes, the motor moves only slightly, it suggests that the problem is mechanical, either due to binding or breakage, or due to hairs and fluff wound round the axles and bearings. If there is no sign of life in the motor when the wires are applied

and the brushes are in good condition, then it would appear to be the motor which is at fault and you will need to take the model to your local dealer for attention.

The best way of maintaining your model railway in good working order, with a minimum of effort, is to carry out the necessary servicing and repairs regularly. If you set aside part of an operating session each week or two for these jobs you will find that only a short time will usually be required, whereas if you let too many jobs accumulate, you will be in for a long session when you eventually get round to attending to them. In the meantime your railway will not be running as well as it should.

Some modellers like to keep a notebook to list any faults which they notice during operating sessions so that they do not forget them when they have a maintenance and repair session. One system which has advantages, especially on a large layout with several operators, is to have some way of marking points on the track at which derailments occur and the locomotives or stock concerned. If several markers accumulate at one point on the track it suggests that there is a fault here and that the derailments were not just unlucky isolated incidents. Similarly, if one engine or wagon collects several markers it would seem that a careful check for the fault is indicated. The necessary repairs or adjustments to the track, locomotives or wagons can then be carried out.

Maintenance

Exhibiting your layout

I am always impressed by the number of model railway exhibitions which are staged, mostly by the many clubs and societies throughout the country, each year. Though some of these shows are disappointing because of poor choice of layouts or bad organisation, most are successful and provide a great deal of pleasure and entertainment, both for model railway enthusiasts and for other members of the general public who visit the shows. It can also be very enjoyable and satisfying for the railway modeller to participate in such exhibitions by showing his or her own layout.

To provide the greatest possible interest the organisers should try to bring together a good variety of different types of layouts, large and small, of differing prototypes, standard and narrow gauge, of different scales, and so on. They should also try to achieve a reasonable balance so that all the visitors will find something of particular interest to them. It is also desirable that the organisers should ensure that all the layouts are of a good standard and that they have not appeared in the same area too often without alterations or additions

having been made. When members of the public are paying for entry I do feel that they have a right to expect that the layouts on display will not be inferior and will not be largely the same ones as at the previous show! It is also important for the club in question in the long term, both for recruitment and for success in staging future shows, that the standards be kept up.

In general the layouts shown fall into two categories, personal and club layouts. The former are usually designed and built purely for the owners' enjoyment and the idea of exhibiting only arises much later. However, some individual modellers have constructed personal layouts with shows in mind. In some cases lack of space at home makes it difficult to operate a model railway and they concentrate more on construction there, taking the opportunity to indulge in some interesting operation while at exhibitions. An example of such a model is Keith Gowen's 'Market Redwing' TT-gauge branch line layout which has been regularly and successfully exhibited in recent years. Keith has little space for a layout

Below A view of Keith Gowen's TT-gauge branch line layout which was built for exhibition use. **Right** *A scene on the Bridport branch OO-gauge layout built by the Model Group of the Brooklands Railway Society. Note the effective backscene which not only makes the layout appear larger but also serves to conceal the operators. The road overbridge neatly hides the exit of the track through the backscene to reach the fiddle yard.* **Below right** *A neatly lettered name board completes the exhibition presentation of the Brooklands Railway Society Model Group OO-gauge Bridport branch layout.*

at home so he planned his model railway for exhibition use. The layout was designed so that the four sections which make it up are easy to transport and assemble, and so that they can be conveniently stored in a large cupboard at his home when not in use.

Club layouts are often built specifically for exhibition use by the members. Whether or not the layout was designed for show purposes there are some points to be considered. The layout should be an operating model railway and it should work well. There is a place for static models at exhibitions but layouts should be seen in action. It is preferable that the layout should appear to be complete even if further work is, in fact, still to be carried out later. So, if you have been invited to exhibit your layout this is a good reason for completing any areas of scenery that are as yet unfinished, for building any missing structures, and for adding figures and other details to bring your layout to completion. A possible exception is if you have a particular construction method, for example for scenery, and you wish to show

how this is carried out, perhaps as a series of step by step stages. However, this would probably be best shown as a separate static display in conjunction with your layout, rather than leaving parts of the layout unfinished.

When a layout is on show the presentation is important. Though the surface of the layout may have been properly coloured, detailed and finished, the edges, the framing of the baseboard, may have been left as bare wood. If so a better appearance will result if these edges, after any necessary filling and sanding, are painted with matt black paint. This gives a neat but unobtrusive finish. If your layout lacks a scenic background consider installing one. It will give an impression of greater depth and realism to your scenery and, if you will be operating from behind the layout, the backscene will partly conceal you from the viewers. A backdrop can also be useful for hiding a fiddle yard from view.

Also part of the presentation is a neat name board for your railway. You may also like to provide some explanatory information about

58

the layout and perhaps a track plan. If your model is based on a particular prototype line, for example a branch line, you might like to feature a display of photographs of the real thing to show visitors what you have modelled. If you are running the layout to a timetable or are following a sequence of operation during the exhibition you may wish to have a copy of the timetable mounted beside the layout so that members of the public can follow the movements that are taking place at any particular time. Prior to the show you will probably be asked to provide some details of your layout and perhaps a track plan for inclusion in the official printed exhibition guide or handbook. Try to cover the things which you would like to know about the layout if it belonged to someone else when you write these brief notes about the model.

If you are invited to show your layout at an exhibition, check on its transportability well before the date of the show. Can it be carried in sections in a car or estate car or will it be necessary to borrow or hire a small van? If you own a car and are planning to build a layout it may be worth while designing it in sections

The Mid Hants Model Railway Group model of the Watlington branch in EM gauge is a portable layout and many of the small details, such as the human figures and the telegraph pole in this view of the station approach, together with the structures, are detachable for storage and transport.

which will fit into your car. If you do not take your layout down very often, try a few practice runs of taking the sections apart and reassembling them so that the process will be quick and easy when you come to set it up at the show. Constructing the layout so that fragile items such as structures and details can be removed for transportation or storage will help to avoid damage. If you do this keep the removable items in boxes or cartons so that they do not get mislaid when not on the layout. The Mid Hants Model Railway Group's exhibition model of the Watlington Branch in EM gauge is a portable layout on which almost all the structures and details, such as telegraph poles, lamps, figures, road vehicles, and so on, can be removed for moving or storing the layout. Each human figure has a wire fitted beneath one foot which fits into a suitably placed hole in the platform or other surface. It is also important to have some means of carrying your locomotives and rolling stock safely to and from the exhibition. This may simply be a cardboard box within which the individual models are placed after wrapping in tissue paper or after putting into their original boxes. If you anticipate attending a number of shows it is worth taking the time to make a wooden carrying case fitted with partitions in appropriate positions and lined with foam rubber to protect the models.

It is a good idea to keep the electrical arrangements for your layout as neat and tidy as possible. This will make it easier to set up and there will be less risk of people getting snagged by the wiring with the danger of disconnecting or damaging it. As you may need assistance from club members in running your layout, particularly when you want to have a break so that you can have a meal or visit the rest of the show, it is helpful if your control arrangements are straightforward and clearly labelled. Thus another operator taking over will be able to run the layout without too much difficulty and without the need for elaborate instructions.

At some exhibitions the lighting is poor. Often the hall is a hired one, not equipped with suitable lighting and there may be little the club can do to provide better illumination. Poor lighting may make it difficult for the visitors to see the detail work on your layout properly and can also give the impression that it is dull and lifeless instead of doing justice to your realistic colouring. It is well worth while fitting effective lights to your layout if you plan to attend a few exhibitions; the lights may also be useful when running the model railway at home. Effective lighting can do a great deal to enhance a model railway but it is an aspect of presentation that

Above *Dick Wyatt has several bright lights which he fixes above the corners of his narrow-gauge layout at shows. These enable the beautifully detailed and coloured scenery and structures to be seen to full advantage. These two pictures were taken at an exhibition and the excellent even illumination is evident.* **Below** *The control panel of the Mid Hants Model Railway Group EM-gauge model of Watlington station is neatly laid out and fully labelled, making it easy for operators, even those who do not regularly run the layout.*

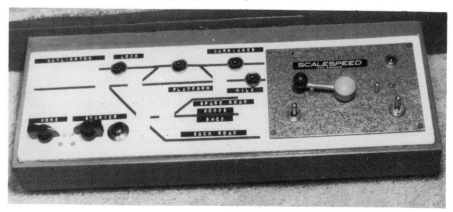

Exhibiting your layout

Plate glass or perspex panels provide effective protection for a layout at shows without interfering with viewing, as on this exhibition layout owned by Hestair Models. The top edge of the screen is just visible in this picture as a white line across the lower part.

is often rather neglected. As a temporary exhibition measure even a couple of adjustable reading lamps can be of use on a small layout if positioned to illuminate important parts of the model. An ideal arrangement is to fit fluorescent strip lighting over your layout as this gives even illumination, but this is more suitable for home use than at exhibitions.

At shows there are inevitably visitors usually, though not always, children, who seemingly must touch everything, including your layout, with the risk of damage to small details. Efforts are made at exhibitions to keep the public from getting too close to the layouts, often by putting a row of chairs in front of each layout. This can be reasonably effective but it is difficult to stop children from moving or climbing onto the chairs. If you are planning to attend several shows as an exhibitor you may feel it is worth the effort and cost of fitting perspex panels along the front edge of the layout. These panels of perspex, thick enough to be rigid, should be about 10 or 12 inches high and are very effective in preventing handling of the layout by the public but do not interfere with viewing. They are best fixed in place with screws along the lower edges so that they can be fitted for shows but easily removed when the layout is again set up at home.

Operating models such as cranes, windmills, watermills, and so on seem popular with visitors to model railway shows and you might consider installing one or more on your layout.

Some modellers feel that models of this type are inappropriate on a scale model railway layout, regarding them as gimmicky and toy-like. However the kits available are generally well detailed and realistic models and the extra movement and interest which these working models can add to the scene are of benefit, particularly on a small layout where the train operating potential may be rather limited.

I have already mentioned that it is important to check and prepare the locomotives, rolling stock and track on your layout beforehand so that operation will be as smooth and reliable as possible during the exhibition. Conditions at shows are often unfavourable because of dust and dirt, humidity, and so on. If the show lasts more than one day it is a good idea to clean the track before starting operation each day.

Rather than run the trains at random it is much better to have some system of operation for exhibitions. Haphazard running of the trains may give a toy-like impression to the visitors whereas systematic operation will create a much more realistic effect. Rather than have to decide what you are going to do on the spur of the moment, have a simple sequence arranged and practised beforehand. Try to make this series of train movements interesting and authentic so that visitors will find them realistic and will want to see what happens next. Keep the sequence fairly simple and make sure that you are really familiar with it so that with the distractions of the exhibition you can still remember what you are doing and what you

Above *Operating models add interest and are particularly beneficial on a small layout. This interesting working lift bridge was built from a Pola/Hornby kit. The bridge spans the entrance to a small harbour on an 00-gauge layout.* **Below** *A scene on the Bridport branch 00-gauge layout built by the Model Group of the Brooklands Railway Society. The attractive scenery has been realistically blended with the back scene giving a very spacious effect. Note the card system indicating to viewers the train movements which are taking place. As each is completed the card is flipped over to reveal the next.*

should do next! It is helpful to have a card or a series of cards on which the moves are clearly printed to use as an aid to memory and for the benefit of any assistants or relief operators who are not familiar with operating the layout. The interest of your model railway for the viewers will be enhanced if it is made clear to those watching what train movements are taking place. A convenient method is to have a series of cards with the moves on them. These cards are mounted in a suitable place arranged so that, as each move is completed, the card concerned can be flipped up to reveal the next. Keith Gowen uses this scheme with a convenient variation. In addition to the information on the front of each card intended for the viewer, there are details on the rear for the operator. Any sequence should not be too long so that it can be completed reasonably quickly. There can then be a pause before it is repeated. During this natural break spectators will move away making room for others to take their places to see the layout in action. Equally important, it gives an opportunity for visitors to ask questions and to talk to the operators.

Exhibitions have an important role to play in public relations for railway modelling in encouraging people to take up the hobby and

Opposite *Two views of Graham Lindley's attractive 009-gauge 'Lydd Valley' layout. The track plan includes a through station and hidden sidings used as a fiddle yard. The layout is designed to link up with one built by a friend for exhibition purposes.* **This page** *The Greenwich & District NGRS 009-layout provides excellent publicity for the preserved 2 foot 3 inch gauge Talyllyn Railway in Mid Wales.* **Above** *The Wharf Station is an accurate replica of the prototype, complete even to the locomotive and slate wagon on static display outside the museum building.* **Below** *Pendre, where the sheds and workshops are situated, is not an exact model but does capture the atmosphere of the real thing.*

in helping less experienced modellers. You will find this contact very interesting, enjoyable and satisfying and often you can pick up new ideas and information yourself. If there is some particular feature of your layout which is unusual or of special interest you may find that there are numerous comments and questions about it. For example, Graham Lindley has found that so many visitors are interested in the method of modelling grass on his 009 Lydd Valley layout that he now takes a sample of the grass matting he used to show to those visitors who enquire about the construction technique.

An idea which has great potential, but which has been little exploited so far, is the use of a taped commentary to accompany and explain the operation of the layout. Not only does this indicate to the audience what movements are taking place and why, making operation more interesting for them, but the commentary can also be a useful guide for the operator. The idea has much to recommend it, particularly as so many modellers must surely own or have access to cassette recorders now. The only modeller that I know of who has employed this technique is the Reverend Awdry, well known not only for his railway modelling but also for his very popular children's books. If the large crowd gathered around his layout throughout the show is any indication, the commentary was very popular with the visitors!

Models are always very effective in attracting public interest and attention and the railway preservation societies are finding that models of stations on their lines are an excellent form of publicity. Not only can the model show the station or line as it is today but it can also show planned future developments, and in a much more effective way than plans or drawings.

In this way the general public can get a very clear idea of what the society is trying to achieve and they are more likely to support the preservation and restoration work with donations or with offers of voluntary work. If you are a member of one of the preservation societies a very interesting and useful project for you to undertake could be the modelling of part of the railway for exhibition purposes.

Railway modelling is a hobby and the important thing is to enjoy your participation. For your own personal modelling you should feel that you can please yourself what you do. It should not become a chore and, if you do not feel like modelling at any particular time, then you should give it a miss. However, when you agree to show your layout you have a commitment to be ready on time and to put on a good show. You should not back out without very good reason as the organisers are depending on you. Be sure when you agree to attend that all the details of where and when the exhibition will be held are clear. Check on whether you will be paid expenses for travelling, if accommodation has been arranged if necessary, and so on.

Modellers often do not realise the value of their layouts and of their locomotives and rolling stock, having built them up gradually, and are particularly prone to underestimate the amount of work which would be involved in replacement. When exhibiting your layout the risks of theft, damage or loss are inevitably increased and it is important to consider the matter of insurance. Sometimes the exhibition organisers arrange insurance cover for all the models involved but you should check on this and, if none is provided, consider obtaining your own.

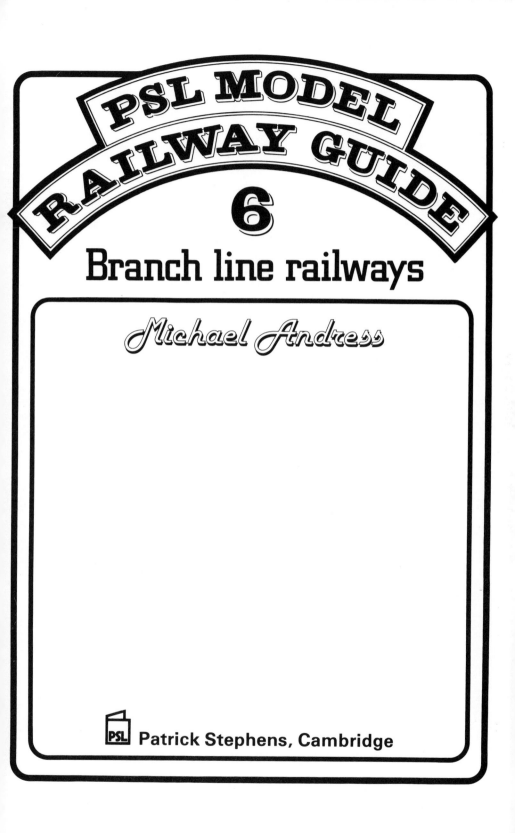

PSL MODEL RAILWAY GUIDE

6

Branch line railways

Michael Andress

PSL Patrick Stephens, Cambridge

Softbound edition first published March 1981

Combined casebound edition (with *PSL Model Railway Guide 5*) first published May 1983

British Library Cataloguing in Publication Data

Andress, Michael
    Model railway guide.
    6: branch line railways
    1. Railroads — Models
    I. Title
    625.1'9'0223   TF197

    ISBN 0-85059-437-5 (softbound)
    ISBN 0-85059-618-1 (combined casebound)

Also in the same series and by the same author
1 Baseboards, track and electrification
2 Layout planning
3 Structure modelling
4 Scenery
5 Operating your layout
7 Modern railways
8 Narrow gauge railways

Cover photograph by Brian Monaghan

Text photoset in 8 on 9 pt Univers by Manuset Limited, Baldock, Herts. Printed in Great Britain on 90 gsm Fineblade coated cartridge and bound, by The Garden City Press, Letchworth, Herts, for the publishers Patrick Stephens Limited, Bar Hill, Cambridge, CB3 8EL, England.

Contents

Introduction   4
Prototype branches   6
Why model branch lines?   8
Advantages and disadvantages   11
Layout schemes   15
Locomotives and rolling stock   23
Structures and scenery   26
Operation   29
Further developments   30
Other types of branches   32
Research   35
Layouts   37
Layout ideas   52

Introduction

Railway modelling is perhaps the most popular of all constructional hobbies and part of the attraction must surely be the very wide scope which the hobby offers. Though I have dabbled in various other modelling hobbies I have yet to find one which has such diversity of construction and operation. Much of the lasting appeal of modelling railways comes from the fact that, after we have built or bought models which are accurate replicas of the real locomotives and rolling stock, we can run them in a manner which realistically duplicates the operation of prototype railways. Because we do not just have models of individual locomotives, coaches, wagons, structures and so on, but create a whole unified system, the model railway is much more interesting. In addition the layout will be different from that constructed by any other modeller even though

many of the individual parts may be the same. Thus one creates one's own unique model railway and this increases the satisfaction and enjoyment of the hobby.

For the many beginners who take up railway modelling each year a very important step is the construction of their first scale model railway layout. Ideally, this should be a layout which will be interesting to build and operate but which will not demand too much in the way of skill, time and money so that there is every chance of it being successfully completed before the initial enthusiasm and interest are lost

An excellent choice is a branch line model. Such a layout will give the novice the opportunity to try out all aspects of construction work — baseboard building, tracklaying, structure modelling, scenery construction,

An attractive branch line scene modelled in 4 mm scale by Terry Jenkins. The typical GWR halt station is a John Day Models plastic kit and the locomotive is the Airfix 1400 Class 0-4-2T.

and, if he or she wishes, locomotive and rolling stock modelling — in a small area and at relatively little cost. When completed the model railway can be operated in a realistic and authentic manner. Thus a branch line layout can provide useful experience in construction together with continued operating enjoyment.

In this book my aim is to introduce the subject of branch line modelling to the beginner and to point out some of the advantages and disadvantages of such a choice. I also want to look at typical arrangements for branch line layouts and to consider the alternatives of accurately following a specific prototype and of merely basing the model more generally on one company or area. A selection of branch line layouts in various popular scales are included to show the reader how different modellers have tackled the subject and to give the beginner ideas for his or her own layout. Finally I have taken three prototype branch lines which are still in operation today to show how each could be used as the basis of a layout. Alternatively features from them could be included in other layouts.

The ideas and information presented here are not for the most part new or original but are based on the work of many modellers, the development of branch line modelling to its present state having taken place over a period of some 30 years. Because an idea devised by one person may be modified, developed and improved by others it is often difficult to know just who first thought up any particular scheme. Modellers such as the late John Ahern (Madder Valley Railway), the Reverend Peter Denny (Buckingham Branch) and Maurice Deane (Culm Valley Branch) have been leaders in branch line modelling and I am grateful to them for the information, enjoyment and inspiration I have received from reading about their models. Much credit is also due to Cyril Freezer, now Editor of *Model Railways* magazine. As the idea of modelling branch lines has developed he has presented the concepts involved with clarity and enthusiasm and his many excellent layout plans based on these principles are ideal for the modeller wanting to build a layout of this type.

I would like to thank all those modellers who have kindly allowed me to use photographs of their work to illustrate this book. In particular I am grateful to Graham Bailey, Harold Bowcott, Alan Copas, Allan Downes, Keith Gowen, Terry Jenkins, Betty Kay, the members of the Mid Hants Model Railway Group, Brian Monaghan and Mike Sharman. I would also like to thank John Brewer, Editor of *Railway Modeller* magazine, for permission to reproduce the photographs of Harold Bowcott's layout.

Prototype branches

We should perhaps, at this early stage, decide just what we mean by a branch line, both in general prototype terms and in the more limited definition usually applied for modelling purposes. Strictly speaking a branch line is any line which diverges from the main line and this category includes even major routes. These latter are double tracked, and in appearance and in operation are virtually identical to the main line. As on the main route the trains will be long and hauled by heavy locomotives.

However, when we speak of modelling branch lines we usually refer to the short, single track, country branch serving a small seaside or country town, perhaps with one or more small intermediate stations or halts. Such lines proliferated in those optimistic days when the railway network was spreading over the whole country and when every small town was anxious to be linked to the railway system for the increased trade and prosperity it was hoped would result. Some of these branches were built by the many small independent companies which were formed and were later taken over by the larger concerns; others were backed from the outset by the main line companies. Many of the branches were successful and profitable, especially when there were local trades and industries to provide traffic and where the new line formed the most convenient link to the main routes

enabling passengers and produce to reach their destinations easily. For other lines it was a struggle for survival from the beginning. Often the stations were built to be large enough to cope with the amount of traffic the promoters optimistically assumed would develop, but which in many cases did not. At seaside towns and in holiday areas facilities were provided for the peak traffic of the summer period but the income from this was not sufficient to make up for the lack of passengers during the rest of the year.

Though the branch line closures from the 'Beeching Axe' were the most dramatic and most familiar to the general public they were by no means the first. The best years for these lines were before the First World War and there has been a steady decline since then. The increasing numbers of cars, lorries and buses appearing on the roads provided competition for the railways and the branch lines were particularly affected. For reasons of economy some stations had been built at a distance from the towns and villages they served so that passengers had a long walk at the end of their rail journey. The bus could offer a much more convenient service at a lower fare. Thus even in the 1920s many lines had already had to cut back on their services, and there were many closures in the 1930s. After the Second World War British Railways continued to reduce

Rural branch line atmosphere preserved at Buckfastleigh on the Dart Valley Railway where a train waits to leave for Totnes. (Photograph by David Andress.)

country branch line services and this was later accelerated with the policies of rationalisation and economy.

Those branches which survived these cutbacks were streamlined for greater efficiency and economy. Sidings, passing loops and any other now unnecessary tracks have been lifted, and in some cases the line has been kept open only as far as one of the intermediate stations. On some branches traffic is now limited to passengers and the goods facilities have been closed. Other branches have been kept open for bulk freight of some type but the unprofitable passenger services have been abandoned. The lines which still carry passengers usually do so in diesel or electric multiple units (DMUs or EMUs) and there have been big reductions in staffing.

The great disadvantage of modern branch lines from the modelling point of view is the very limited operational scope, and ideally the lines are best modelled in the days of steam, preferably at a time when there was still a good deal of traffic, both passenger and goods, so that operation will be interesting. The most suitable choice for the beginner is the short, single track, feeder branch line, the classic country branch. However, if more space is available, the longer single track branch with its intermediate stations, longer trains, greater variety of locomotives and rolling stock and more interesting timetable, has much to offer. Another type of branch line, also interesting but less often modelled, is the cross country link between two main routes. These branches may be single or double track and while some have only light traffic, others are more similar to a main line in their operation. Suburban branches are rarely modelled; most are still in use but are now operated with DMUs or EMUs. Traffic can be intensive but such lines are more suited to the experienced modeller rather than the beginner. A further category of branch line is the industrial branch, built to serve one or a number of industries.

Surviving branch lines now employ diesel or electric multiple units for passenger services. This two-coach EMU was photographed recently on the Lymington Branch (Southern Region) between the Pier and Town stations.

Traffic on such lines may be almost entirely limited to one type of bulk load, coal, iron ore, clay, oil and so on, or may be mixed, with the line serving a variety of different industries or a dock area. Though the country branch is usually regarded as the best choice for the modeller, particularly the beginner, one of the smaller industrial branches can also be a good basis for an interesting layout.

There are many books covering various aspects of prototype branch lines. Most of these describe particular branches or areas and are invaluable if you are modelling the line concerned. However there are also some more general books which will give the reader a good idea of how the branch lines came into being, what they were like in their heyday, how they operated and how they changed over the years. Younger readers who did not have the opportunity to visit the lines in steam days will find that these books can give them some of the atmosphere and feel of the country branches. Older readers will enjoy the memories the books bring back! Three books I have found interesting and informative are *Branch Lines* by O.S. Nock, *British Branch Lines* by H.A. Vallance and *The Country Railway* by David St John Thomas. The first two are out of print, though I have seen them both on sale second hand recently so you may come across them. You should certainly be able to borrow them through your local library. Though such books may not provide any specific information that you will need for your own layout, reading them will give you a familiarity with the subject and will fill in the background in a way which will help you to create a realistic branch line layout.

Prototype branches

Why model branch lines?

In the early days of railway modelling the emphasis was very much on the locomotives, rolling stock and track, with lineside features limited to a few structures such as station buildings and platforms, signal boxes and engine sheds. The 'scenery' was often no more than a railway poster or two behind the tracks. The rest was provided by the enthusiast's imagination which also allowed him to run main line trains of only three or four coaches to a 'Euston' with only two platforms quite happily! During the 1940s with the increasing popularity of 00 scale and under the influence of various modellers of whom John Ahern was outstanding, the idea of creating a realistic miniature landscape for the railway to run through and serve became widely accepted. This emphasis on realism also meant that the caricature of a main line terminus with platforms only long enough for three coach trains had to go!

Because we are modelling a whole system rather than just a few separate items which could be displayed on shelves or in a cabinet we must find space to accommodate our layout. The problem of finding adequate space is often emphasised but there are other factors which must also be taken into account. To complete a model railway there are many models to be constructed or purchased and time and money will be required. Thus when planning a layout we must consider not only the space available to accommodate it but also the amount of time and money we can afford and how long a period we are prepared to let the construction of the layout take. Obviously there is no point in planning a large and complex system if there is space for only a very small layout. What is often less evident to the beginner is the heavy commitment in hours of work and in cost involved in the building of a large model railway. It is essential not to be too ambitious in the choice of a first layout.

If we want to build a model railway that is as realistic as possible within these restrictions of space and of outlay in terms of time and money we must look for a suitable prototype. The country branch line, especially in the days of steam, has much to recommend it as a choice. The passenger trains often consisted of only two or three coaches pulled by a small tank engine, or were short push-pull trains, so that we can model trains of realistic length even on a small layout. Goods trains were also short but often had an interesting variety of rolling stock. Station layouts were usually fairly simple with only a limited number of points permitting economy both in space and in the cost of the trackwork. An attractive branch line type of layout can be developed easily from the train set and it can be an ideal first permanent scale layout with considerable scope for attractive scenery and structures.

During the 1950s the branch line model railway concept was developed considerably. At that time the idea was not so much to provide a suitable subject for beginners as to enable more experienced modellers to create a model railway which would look realistic and operate in an authentic manner within the confines of a small space. The short prototype trains allowed the modeller to run scale length trains despite the small size of his layout. Because the station track layouts are simple on branch lines they can be compressed to fit onto a model railway while still retaining their essential features so that the model can be operated according to prototype practice and following a proper timetable.

Because the aim was realistic operation, the point-to-point track arrangement, which represents the prototype railway running from one town to another, was generally preferred to the continuous run schemes typical of the train set. To provide the greatest interest in the least possible space, attention was concentrated on the branch line terminus and the now classic branch line terminus to fiddle yard design was developed. The fiddle yard consists of hidden sidings representing the rest of the railway system and on which trains can be rearranged by hand. Such a track plan can be fitted onto baseboards of various shapes but a popular arrangement is on two narrow baseboards

The atmosphere of a country branch line terminus, together with the village it serves, faithfully captured in miniature by the expert modelling of Allan Downes. The superbly realistic buildings were all scratch-built. The scale is 4 mm to the foot. (Photographs by Brian Monaghan.)

joined to form an L shape and often fitted into the corner of a room. This design has the advantage of giving the greatest running possibilities in a minimum area and often a layout of this shape can be accommodated in a room whereas a conventional rectangular baseboard would not be acceptable as it would block the centre of the room too much.

When the idea of modelling a branch line terminus was first put forward there was very little in the way of ready-to-run equipment and kits available. Thus the choice of a layout for which relatively little track and few points were required and which could be operated realistically with only one locomotive, two or three coaches and a few wagons meant that, even though most of the items needed had to be hand built, the layout could be completed within a reasonable length of time. In the years since then there has been a dramatic change in the availability of ready-to-run models and kits and in the standards of accuracy and detail of these models. Nowadays the beginner can go into a model railway stockist and buy off the shelf the locomotives needed for a branch line layout without difficulty, especially in 00 scale. The models will be inexpensive but will run well, and the accuracy to scale and degree of detailing will be better than any but an expert scratchbuilder could achieve. The ready availability also of assembled points and flexible track of excellent quality and of easily made up structure kits means that even a beginner can fairly quickly bring a layout of this type to the stage where it is interesting to operate and view. The country setting allows the modeller to add simple but attractive scenery to complete the model.

Great Western branches are particularly popular and are very well catered for wit commercial models but other prototypes ca also be followed just as successfully though little more work on the part of the modelle may be required. Because so many enthusias have constructed branch line model railwa layouts, the majority being based on Gre Western Railway prototypes, there have bee suggestions from time to time that the subje has become hackneyed and that modelle should choose other prototypes or anoth form of railway to model. Fortunately a railway modelling is a hobby you are free to d just as you wish. For those who want to mod something a little different there is plenty choice. However, if you like the idea of a Grea Western Railway branch line do not be put o by such comments. The great popularity of th particular subject can be seen as a measure how successful a choice it has been for mar modellers and as an indication that it is likely be for you also. Because the GWR is the mo popular it has the greatest variety of ready-t run and kit models available, making it easier have an interesting layout with a varie locomotive roster and selection of rollir stock.

However, conversely, do not be talked int modelling a branch line because of the eas and convenience, or because of limited spac if you do not like branch lines. To produce good layout, one which will provide the mo interest and enjoyment for you the builder ar operator, you must choose a subject you lik and for which you feel an affinity and interes Never build something just because you fe you should as the modelling will become chore. There are alternatives to a branch lir model suitable for even the smallest spaces.

Advantages and disadvantages

have already mentioned a number of advant-
ges which a branch line layout can offer but it
ight now be convenient to sum these up.
lso, inevitably with any compromise, such as
almost always necessary with a model rail-
ay, there are some disadvantages and we can
onsider these here as well.

The key feature of a branch line layout is that
offers realistic operation and appearance in a
inimum space. Because the layout is small it
an be completed within a limited budget, both
terms of money and of the time the modeller
an devote to construction. It is simple so
ould not be beyond the skill and knowledge
the novice. As the amount of track is limited
is relatively easy to lay it all accurately and
moothly so that good running can be
chieved and the small size of the layout will
ean that maintenance can be easily and
uickly carried out. For these reasons a branch
ne layout is particularly suitable for the begin-
er, especially the young modeller. Such a lay-
ut can be fitted conveniently into a bedroom
ithout interfering with sleeping, studying and
o on and, if necessary, it can be constructed
o that it is portable, enabling it to be moved
nd stored without difficulty.

The usual design employed means that the
yout can be extended easily by the addition
f further sections or can be incorporated into
larger layout later. Alternatively, once it has
een completed and has provided entertain-
ent, both in construction and operation, it
an be scrapped without the loss of too much
utlay in time and money. It will have more
an paid for itself in the enjoyment and
xperience it has given the modeller and, of
ourse, many of the purchased items such as
ack, structures, locomotives and rolling stock
an be reused on later layouts. It may even be
ossible to use the baseboards again.

The disadvantages of a branch line layout
ainly relate to its limitations in scope, both in
e amount of construction work which can be
arried out and in the operational possibilities.
he modeller may find that all too soon there is
ttle more that can be built, though we will

look later in this book at ways in which we can
extend this even on a very small layout. The
operational limitations are perhaps even more
significant as only a simple timetable can be
worked and once this has been repeated a
number of times interest may well wane.

A failing of the classic branch line scheme of
terminus to fiddle yard is that the latter, which
may be almost half the layout, is hidden from
view. Thus on an already small layout, the
visible part, the section which is of most
interest, is even further limited in size.

However, if extension of the layout is
possible the disadvantages can be overcome.
Building new sections for the model keeps up
the construction interest and, of course, operation becomes more complicated and
entertaining as the layout is made larger. A fine
example of a branch line layout which began as
a small and simple model but which has been
developed over a period of some 25 years into a
large and extensive model railway is the
Reverend Peter Denny's 'Buckingham Branch'.
If you would like to see the full potential of
branch line modelling I recommend that you
read the excellent account given by the
Reverend Denny in his book *Buckingham
Great Central* published by Peco.

Prototype or freelance

Because of the emphasis on realism in branch
line modelling the beginner may have the initial
impression that the object is to model a particular prototype branch line station exactly to
scale. This is not, however, what is really
intended. Though the layout at many of these
stations was simple the area occupied was
usually considerable and to reproduce the track
arrangement accurately to scale would take
quite a large space. This may well be more than
we have available, and if we should have this
amount of space it could be used more produc-
tively to model a more complex and interesting
station. In fact it is very questionable whether it
would be desirable to model to exact scale
anyway. Though we are fairly meticulous
about scale accuracy with respect to our loco-

Harold Bowcott's 00-scale layout measures 8 ft by 4 ft 9 ins and is hinged to one wall of the room for convenient storage when not in use. This picture shows the layout in the hinged up position. The shelves for storing locomotives and rolling stock are fixed to the wall and fit neatly into the central operating well of the layout. (Photograph by Brian Monaghan, courtesy Railway Modeller.)

motives, rolling stock and generally for the structures, we do not usually model the track layout to scale. Ironically, we may well find that the station would look wrong if we did! There are, I think, two main reasons for this, in effect, optical illusion. First of all we are not used to getting the sort of overall aerial view of the prototype that we have of the model, as we would need to be on a hill or up in a helicopter to do so. We normally look at parts of the prototype station from various ground level positions. Perhaps even more important is the fact that we have become accustomed to seeing some selective compression in model railway layouts and we now regard it as normal and realistic. There is certainly an advantage in this compression, in addition to the space saving, in that it enables us to leave out the relatively uninteresting parts while retaining and bringing more closely together the features we like and which give the prototype, and hence the model, its character and appeal. These departures from exact scale do not mean that the model will not be authentic, merely that we are portraying the atmosphere and workings of a branch line station as an artist would, rather than a surveyor. Another advantage for the single handed operator, and most small layouts should be designed to be conveniently worked by one person even if two or more will operate them from time to

time, is that compressing the track plan in this way will bring all parts of the station within easy reach.

The key feature of branch line stations therefore, is that the simple track arrangements they employ can be compressed significantly without losing their essential characteristics. Such compression is limited by the number of points, as these must be modelled roughly to scale whereas other track can be reduced in length much more easily. Thus the potential compression is much greater for a branch line station with few points than for a main line station with more complex trackwork.

There are several choices open to us in selecting a station to model. We can copy a prototype station as exactly as possible, with some compression of the track plan as necessary or we can base our model on a particular prototype station but adapt it to suit our requirements and interests. Taking this a little further is the idea of modelling an imaginary station based closely on the practice, style and architecture of a specific company or area, perhaps, for example, taking typical Great Western Railway features. Some modellers have applied this idea very successfully to the creation of a station for a branch line which could have existed but which was never built. A fine example is the Reverend Peter Denny's

'Buckingham Branch' for which he created the station which could have been built if the Great Central Railway had reached the real town of Buckingham. Though his line is imaginary it is based accurately on Great Central Railway practice in the year of 1907 for locomotives, rolling stock, structures and details.The fidelity to prototype and period has created an authentic, even though imaginary, model railway.

At the opposite end of the spectrum to the exact model of a particular prototype station is the completely freelance railway, created in its entirety by the modeller and not based on any real railway company. Though this may sound an easy solution in which anything goes and there is no need to bother about research, it is in fact much more difficult to create a convincing model in this way. It has been successfully done but requires considerable knowledge of real railways and also a good deal of imagination and skill to achieve the right effect. The classic example is John Ahern's 'Madder Valley Railway' now on permanent display at Pendon Museum. This expert modeller created his own railway in a realistic but imaginary setting and managed to blend the many diverse prototypes he modelled into a harmonious and balanced whole. He even succeeded in mixing standard-gauge locomotive models in 4 mm scale with narrow-gauge prototypes modelled to a slightly larger scale, all running on the same tracks, without spoiling the effect of realism and authenticity! If you do wish to create a freelance model railway it is important to have a clear idea at the outset of what you are working towards, otherwise there is the danger that the model may become an unrealistic mixture. It is much easier to use a prototype as your guide.

Some modellers have modelled a specific prototype station accurately with successful results. An excellent example is the model of the Watlington Branch built in EM by members of the Mid Hants Model Railway Group, and described in more detail later in this book. This exhibition layout is based very closely on the track layout of the prototype and the structures

Below left *A goods train passes through a cutting realistically modelled from offcuts of softboard broken up and fixed together to give the appearance of rock strata.* (Photo by Brian Monaghan, courtesy *Railway Modeller.*)

Below right *Joypol village on Harold Bowcott's 00-scale layout. Because the maximum depth to permit the layout to fold up against the wall is 9 inches the height of the buildings in the village had to be kept to a minimum and it was not possible to add the chimney pots. The cut out in the top of the backscene at the top left of the photograph is to clear the picture rail and the buildings of the village have been arranged to be clear of the rail. The factory at the right of the scene conceals the controls.* (Photograph by Brian Monaghan, courtesy *Railway Modeller.*)

are all accurate replicas of the real railway buildings at this Oxfordshire terminus. Recreating in miniature a prototype which may have been closed and abandoned years before can be a very satisfying project and of considerable historical interest. If you model a local line you may well find that many people from your area are interested in the layout even though they are not model railway enthusiasts, because they remember the branch as it was in the days of steam. Modelling a specific station in this way may involve you in a good deal of research to find out exactly how it looked at the time your layout will be set. This in itself can be very interesting and can add to the enjoyment of the modelling.

There are, however, some disadvantages to this approach. Such a project does tend to be strictly limited in scope. Once you have completed the track layout as it was in the prototype and have constructed all the buildings and have bought or built suitable locomotives and rolling stock, there is not really any further possibility for development. The timetable operated by the prototype may also be so limited that the model is not very interesting to run.

Another problem is that it may be difficult or impossible to find a prototype which has all the features you would like to include in a model, or one which has sufficient interest to make a good model. Alternatively, if you do find such a prototype it may well be too large for the space you have available.

The ideal solution for the average modeller is either to adapt a particular prototype until it does meet his requirements or to build up a composite station from various desirable features from a number of different prototype stations. Obviously an effort should be made to choose design features, structures and so on which will combine well together. Try also to give a unity to the whole design by basing it on the practice of one company or region.

When it comes to actually designing or selecting a track plan and layout design there is much to be said for the beginner choosing a plan which has been published in a magazine or book. Even though branch line stations and layouts tend to be simple there are pitfalls for the beginner in designing his own. It is important that the layout should permit realistic and interesting operation and that the maximum benefits are obtained from the space which is available. The number of workable arrangements for small layouts is quite limited and all have already been used many times so there is little to be gained in trying to come up

with a completely new and original scheme. The beginner is best advised to take advantage of the experience of the experts and to choose one of their track plans. Many have appeared in the model railway magazines over the year and selections of those which have appeared in *Railway Modeller* magazine have been gathered together by Cyril Freezer into booklets of track plans and have been published by Peco. Of these *60 Plans For Small Railways* in particular includes a number of branch line layouts suitable for the beginner. If you do base your layout on a published track plan there is no reason, of course, why you should not make minor changes to the arrangement of the tracks and other features to suit the space available and your requirements. However, do remember that most of these designs are already as compact as possible so do not try to squeeze them into smaller spaces than those suggested. There is no difficulty, if you have slightly more space than absolutely necessary, in expanding the track plan to fit and the layout will usually be improved by this. The scenic suggestions given on the published plans can be altered to suit your own ideas.

It can be difficult to visualise exactly how a layout will look when constructed from viewing the small scale track plan alone and you may find it helpful to draw the plan out full size before making a decision on whether to build it. The lining paper used beneath wall paper is convenient for this as it comes in rolls and is cheap and easy to obtain. You may also find it useful, particularly if you are redesigning the scenery, to build a small scale model (say 1 inch to 1 foot) of the model railway layout to see how it will appear in three dimensions.

Your choice of layout will be dictated to some extent by the space available. It is advisable, anyway, as I mentioned earlier, to choose something fairly small and simple for a first layout so you can get it to a reasonably complete stage within a relatively short time. Give some thought to the operational possibilities and to the sort of locomotives and rolling stock you would like to run on the layout before making your choice. The geographical setting can generally be wherever you wish. For the most part the track layouts for small stations are similar between different companies and by modelling appropriate scenery and selecting suitable structures and details you can locate your railway anywhere in the country. In the next two sections we can look at some of the designs used for branch line layouts, both the general arrangements for the layouts and the station designs.

Layout schemes

Though there are varied layout designs they tend to conform to a few set patterns. The basic essentials of the classic branch line terminus type of layout are the terminus itself and the fiddle yard to which it is linked. If necessary these can be positioned close together with a minimum of track length between. The yard is usually concealed, at least partly, and the track to it passes through a tunnel mouth, under an overbridge or through some other form of scenic break. The provision of a siding or sidings lying in front of the fiddle yard helps to make it less noticeable, gives extra shunting opportunities and makes some visible use of the part of the layout otherwise taken up by the fiddle yard. A typical small layout of this type was constructed in TT scale by Chris Ellis when he was living in a bedsitter. The track plan is shown here. A small quarry was modelled in front of the fiddle yard adding scenic interest as well as an industrial siding to be shunted.

In an effort to provide space for a more interesting terminus, yet still be able to fit the railway into a small or moderate sized room without preventing other uses of the room, a very significant development took place. The design was bent to an L shape to fit into a corner of the room with the arms extending along the two adjacent walls. This design permitted the maximum of operation and interest in a minimum of space and, in addition, encroached much less onto the room than other designs of the same area would have done. Again, a siding or line to a dock, mine or other feature can be positioned in front of the fiddle yard helping to conceal it and making additional use of the area available. If there is space for it, the terminus to fiddle yard type of layout can easily be extended by adding extra sections between the two ends of the layout. If necessary these additional units can be portable, as can indeed the whole layout, and can be stored away except when actually operating the layout.

If the rectangular format more usually

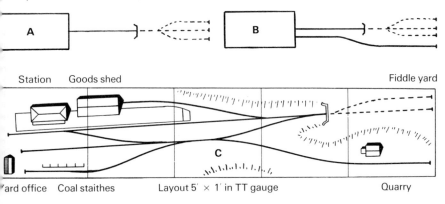

A The basic branch line terminus to fiddle yard scheme. **B** The addition of a siding or sidings in front of the fiddle yard helps to conceal it and also adds to the interest of the layout. **C** Chris Ellis built this TT scale branch line layout in a space of only 5 feet by 1 foot when he was living in a bedsitter. The layout follows the basic arrangement shown in **B** with a quarry siding in front of the fiddle yard.

Station   Goods shed   Fiddle yard

C

Yard office   Coal staithes   Layout 5' × 1' in TT gauge   Quarry

Layout schemes

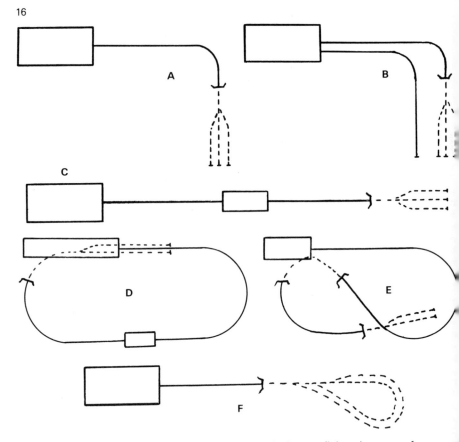

A *The terminus to fiddle yard design can be bent to an L shape to fit into the corner of a room, a very convenient arrangement.* **B** *Again a siding can be positioned in front of the fiddle yard.* **C** *The terminus to fiddle yard scheme lends itself to easy extension by adding extra sections between the terminus and the fiddle yard. The additional section or sections can include one or more intermediate stations and other features of operational or scenic interest.* **D** *If desired the terminus to fiddle yard design can be arranged to fit onto the conventional rectangular baseboard usually employed for the oval type of track plan. Here the fiddle yard is placed beneath the terminus.* **E** *Here a spiral design is employed.* **F** *In N gauge the small radius curves which can be employed enable a reversing loop with one or more holding sidings to be used in place of the usual fiddle yard.*

employed for the oval continuous track arrangement should be preferred, a terminus to fiddle yard design can be accommodated on it successfully by bending it into an oval or spiral shape.

The terminus to fiddle yard scheme was developed with 00 scale in mind but is also suitable for other scales including 0, TT and N. The small radius curves which can be employed in N scale, particularly on hidden sections where realism is not important, means that a different arrangement can be fitted onto the narrow baseboard if desired. Instead of the conventional fiddle yard a reverse loop

together with one or more holding sidings can be utilised.

An interesting alternative to the usual design, first employed I believe by Maurice Deane, is to fit the branch line layout onto a rectangular baseboard with the fiddle yard behind the terminus but concealed from it by a low backscene. This arrangement has two advantages. The modeller can easily reach both the terminus station and the fiddle yard from his operating position in the central well. It also makes it simple to include a link to allow continuous running for locomotives to be run in, or for times when the modeller would like to just sit back and watch the trains in action without the need for any shunting. The link can be concealed so that the realism of the point-to-point scheme is not impaired. This type of layout can also be extended.

Another alternative is to model a through station on a continuous run design. This loses some of the advantages of the terminus design but does make a change from the more typical schemes. If a cross country branch is modelled there is more scope for variety in the choice of locomotives and rolling stock than on a small feeder branch. Part of the oval is concealed and hidden sidings are provided here for use as a fiddle yard.

Station design

The main feature of the typical branch line

G *The Maurice Deane terminus to fiddle yard design with a low backscene separating the two and with a concealed link to allow continuous running.* **H** *This arrangement can also be extended by adding a branch from the oval.* **I** *On a continuous run oval scheme part of the oval can be concealed and hidden sidings provided there for use as a fiddle yard.*

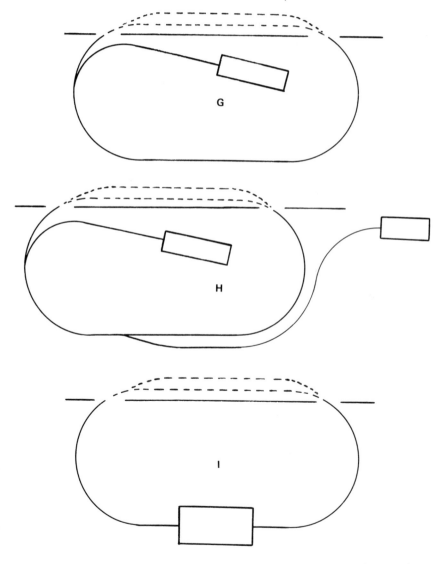

Layout schemes

layout is the station, usually a terminus, less often a through station or junction. Obviously we should make the station as interesting as possible, both in appearance and in operating potential. The scope depends on the space available, and if this is small, the station may have to be very simple, but operation will then be very limited. The accompanying diagrams show a selection of typical station track plans ranging from small to moderate in size, and the layouts described later in the book provide further examples of stations of various types.

If only push-pull passenger trains, railcars or diesel or electric multiple units are employed, a branch line terminus, in its simplest form, need only have the single track with a platform beside it, and in many cases modern branch line termini have been reduced to this form. The train arrives, the driver and guard change positions, and the train departs in the opposite direction. However, such operation is not very interesting for the modeller and it is more usual to provide a run-around loop to enable the engine to reach the other end of the train for the journey back to the junction. The loop can either be placed alongside the platform or can be on the line beyond the platform. In either case it will usually be shared by goods

trains also, these being scheduled to arrive and shunt between passenger trains. At larger stations a separate run-around loop may be provided for goods trains. The loop, or loops, must, of course, be long enough to hold the trains and there must also be sufficient room on the track beyond it for the locomotive. For 00 eight inches will usually be adequate for the small engines typically used on branch lines, though it would be worthwhile checking on the lengths of any locomotives which you plan to run on your layout.

The platform can be single with tracks on one or both sides. An attractive arrangement is to have a shorter bay at one side which can be used for a railcar, or for vans for milk, parcels and mail. An alternative is to have a platform each side of the two tracks with a release crossover forming a run-around formation. If desired, a shorter bay can be provided, in addition, at one side. At a junction station one line can curve away and a platform between it and the straight track can serve both. In general it is worth noting that a slightly curved platform is more attractive in model form than the more usually chosen straight type.

Goods facilities can be very simple, with trains sharing the run-around loop with

Typical branch line terminus station track plans. (Not to scale.) **A** *A very simple terminus with run-around loop and two sidings, one for a small goods shed, the other for engine coal and water.* **B** *Another small station with goods shed and coal staithes.* **C** *Passenger traffic is more important at this small terminus with two platforms for passengers with a bay platform for milk and parcels. There is a single goods siding with goods shed.* **D** *In this design the run-around loop is on the line before the station platform. Facilities include goods shed, coal staithes and an engine shed with coal and water.* **E** *This larger terminus has a siding serving a nearby factory. There is a two track engine shed while the goods shed and goods platform serves two sidings.* **F** *A larger terminus serving a small port. In addition to the run-around loop for the station itself there is a second run-around loop for the sidings for the wharf and the oil depot so that shunting can be carried on here without blocking the main line or the station.*

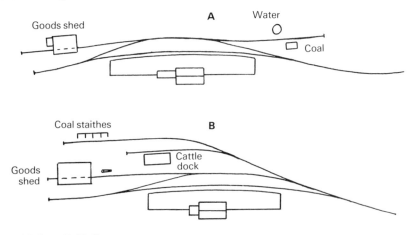

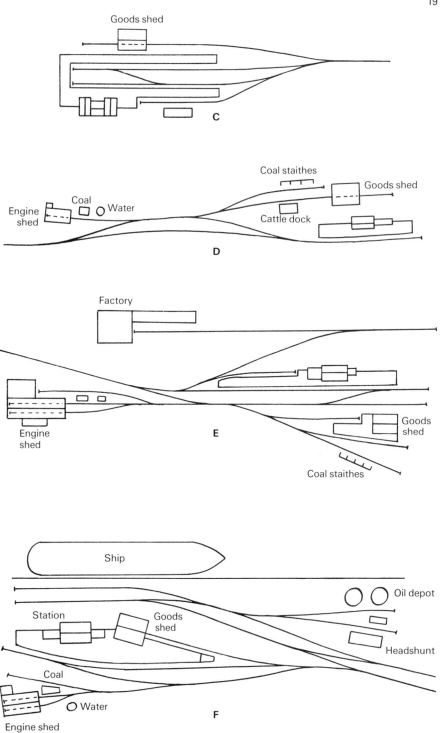

Layout schemes

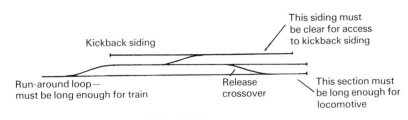

Kickback siding

This siding must be clear for access to kickback siding

Run-around loop — must be long enough for train

Release crossover

This section must be long enough for locomotive

A run-around loop with a siding and a kick back siding.

passenger trains, and with only one or two sidings. If extra sidings can be included, operation will be more interesting as additional facilities can be provided. Typically, a small terminus may have a goods shed, coal staithes and a cattle dock. If a siding to a small factory, a dairy, a wharf, or some other source of extra traffic can also be fitted in, so much the better. At larger stations there may be more sidings and a headshunt may be included so that shunting can be carried out without interfering with the arrival and departure of passenger trains. A separate run-around loop for goods trains will also increase the operational flexibility of the station.

When planning sidings and loops try to avoid reverse or 'S' curves as these may cause problems in running, and even derailments. Kick-back sidings are sometimes included on a model railway layout. Access to one of these is only possible if the siding from which it leads is empty already or is cleared at the time. Because of this the modeller may find that he does not use the kick-back siding as he does not want to be bothered with carrying out the extra moves required. Conversely, however, we can take the view that anything which involves more shunting movements adds to the operating activity and makes the layout more interesting. It is a matter of personal choice whether you want to keep operation simple and easy or to make it as complex as you can. Modellers who particularly enjoy shunting may choose to include one or more kick-back sidings on their layouts because of the complications they introduce. Provided the modeller is prepared to shunt them, these sidings are convenient from the planning point of view as they often utilise space which cannot be otherwise used.

Engine servicing facilities will also be required. If the engine, or engines, are not shedded at the terminus all that is needed is a small coal stage from which coal is loaded by hand into the bunkers, a water tank and an ash pit. However, it is more interesting to provide a small engine shed as well. This will also give the opportunity to display a second engine on the shed track rather than having to hide it

away in the fiddle yard. A turntable can be installed if tender locomotives are to be operated, but this facility may take up more space than you are able to spare.

To sum up, we should endeavour to make the station as interesting as possible with as many facilities as can be included to give the maximum traffic and operational potential. The more sidings we can provide the more of our rolling stock can be out on show instead of hidden away in the fiddle yard. If we can include an industry or two at the station this will increase the amount and type of goods traffic and also give us the opportunity to model interesting structures. Examples include small factories, a dairy, a timber yard, a wharf or a gas works.

Fiddle yards

As the fiddle yard is an integral component of the classic branch line model railway layout we should perhaps consider in more detail the various forms that this feature may take. The use of these hidden sidings, which represent the rest of the railway system to which our terminus is theoretically linked, enable us to operate our station realistically in a minimum of space. When the idea was first developed modellers provided these tracks with run-arounds and operated the yards very much as a normal station would be. Sometimes a turn-table or sector plate was included at the end of the tracks to allow the engines to be transferred from one line to another and, also with the former, to be turned as well.

However, as the sidings were hidden from view anyway modellers soon found it was easier, quicker and more convenient to ignore prototype practice and merely to provide a bank of storage sidings on which the locomotives and rolling stock could be re-arranged by hand. Hence the name 'fiddle yard'. An alternative to the original scheme of a set of sidings fed by points is the provision of a traverser table with a single track lead, an arrangement which results in a considerable saving in space. The table is moved back and forth to give access to its sidings. The traverser need not be elaborate, all that is needed is a

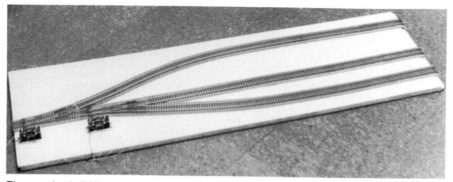

The very simple fiddle yard used with the 00-scale Stonepark Lane branch line terminus layout. In operation a board padded with foam rubber is fitted across the right-hand end to prevent trains running off the sidings.

simple sliding board moved by hand, with spring brass contacts completing the circuit for electrical supply to whichever track is lined up with the entry track. A variant on this device is to have a large sector plate carrying the sidings, as in the fiddle yard constructed by the Mid Hants Model Railway Group for their Watlington Branch layout and illustrated here. This plate pivots so that each of the sidings it carries can be alligned with the entry track. A neat arrangement made with an ordinary small bolt holds the plate in position and ensures that the selected siding is accurately lined up with the entry track.

The Reverend Peter Denny, well known for his superb 4 mm scale Buckingham Branch layout, has made some interesting further develop-ments to fiddle yard design. Finding that the rearrangement of trains in the fiddle yard was proving a rather uninteresting chore for one operator on his model railway, he devised an ingenious detachable five track fiddle yard. The yard has raised sides at each end of which there are grooves into which small end pieces can be slid. When all the trains are in the sidings, the end pieces are fitted into place preventing the trains from rolling off, and the whole yard is detached from the layout, turned end for end, and replaced. This reverses all the trains at once and, as soon as the end pieces are removed, operation can begin again. This is an excellent scheme provided that the trains are fairly short, as they will be on a branch line layout, so that the yard is not too large for easy

This neat sector plate type of fiddle yard constructed by the Mid Hants Model Railway Group for their EM scale Watlington Branch layout saves both on points and on space. This shows the simple but effective method of alignment and locking used.

Mike Sharman built this three-track train turntable for his broad gauge 4 mm scale period exhibition layout. The turntable reverses entire trains and takes the place of a fiddle yard.

handling while turning. A length of four feet should be adequate yet reasonable for handling. For a layout which must be stored away between sessions a convenient arrangement is to house the terminus on top of a chest of drawers, preferably with a cover which hinges up for operating, and to design the fiddle yard to fit as a drawer below. The original style Denny fiddle yard is ideal for this purpose.

I say 'original' because the Reverend Denny has since elaborated on his design to produce an even more ingenious arrangement, which allows reversal without the need for detaching and lifting the yard. With a mechanism based on Meccano parts, the yard is designed to move away a short distance to give clearance after which the whole fiddle yard can be rotated as a train turntable to reverse it. The yard is then moved in again to meet the layout. This fiddle yard is described in detail in an article by Peter Denny in the March 1954 issue of *Model Railway News*. Both the Denny fiddle yard designs combine the benefits of a fiddle yard and a reversing loop but occupy less space than the latter. Mike Sharman, another expert modeller, has recently constructed a train turntable, shown here, for his 4 mm scale broad gauge period exhibition layout, and this is used in a similar way.

When designing a fiddle yard for your layout there are certain points to be considered, no matter which type of yard is chosen. Particularly important, of course, are the number and length of the hidden sidings. While these may be limited by the space available they will also be influenced by the lengths of the trains you plan to operate and the number of trains you will have. These will depend to some extent on the amount of stock you own and on the number of locomotives you have. Train length will also be related to the track arrangements at the station, with the train lengths limited to that which can be accommodated on the run-around loop.

The amount of rearranging by hand which you plan to carry out also has a bearing on the design of a fiddle yard. If you will merely be reversing whole trains on a Denny style fiddle yard you can lay the tracks relatively close together, whereas if you intend to shuffle the stock around extensively in the yard you will need more space between the sidings for convenience and to avoid damage to the locomotives and stock by knocking them over. You may wish to conceal the fiddle yard from view with scenery or structures but you must, of course, take care that it is sufficiently easily accessible for convenient operation, for maintenance and in case of derailments.

Though fiddle yards and hidden sidings are particularly associated with point-to-point lines they can also be usefully employed to add operating potential to layouts based on other track patterns. For example, the rear of an oval can be concealed and sidings can be provided here for train holding or for use as a fiddle yard. Similarly, on an out-and-back scheme, hidden sidings can be led from the reversing loop. As I mentioned earlier, in N scale, where a 180 degree turn can be made in as little as 20 inches of baseboard width, a reversing loop is a feasible alternative to the more usual fiddle yard arrangement employed in 00 scale. If a little more space is available this loop can be combined with hidden sidings giving a more versatile scheme.

Locomotives and rolling stock

One of the advantages of building a branch line layout is that interesting and realistic operation can be carried out with a very limited selection of stock so that the initial financial outlay for locomotives and rolling stock can be very modest. A country branch will typically have one or more small tank engines, though small tender locomotives are also suitable if you prefer. If you use the latter, a turntable can be installed, and will add interest to the engine servicing facilities at the station, if sufficient space is available. However, a turntable is not essential as tender first running was acceptable prototype practice. An occasional through train can provide an excuse to run a larger locomotive if you wish.

The enthusiast is now well catered for in 00 scale; in N scale there is an adequate but more limited selection. For TT scale there are now no ready-to-run British prototype models available and the modeller must build from kits or scratch. In 00 ready-to-run locomotive models include the Airfix GWR 61XX Prairie and 14XX 0-4-2 Tank, the Lima GWR Class 45XX Prairie and Class 94XX 0-6-0 Pannier Tank, the Grafar Class 94XX Pannier 0-6-0 Tank, the Palitoy

Mainline LNER and BR J72 0-6-0 Tank, the Wrenn SR Class R1 0-6-0 Tank and the Hornby GWR Class 57XX 0-6-0 Pannier Tank, among others. The GWR predominance is evident! The Hornby Class M7 0-4-4 Tank, useful for Southern branch line layouts, is unfortunately no longer in production, though may be obtainable second hand. There are also a number of excellent white metal kits from various manufacturers for locomotives suitable for branch lines.

For a GWR branch line of appropriate period, a model of one of the streamlined diesel railcars built in the 1930s and early 1940s would be an interesting addition. K's plan to reintroduce their 4 mm scale kit shortly and a Lima ready-to-run model of Railcar No 22 built at Swindon in 1941 to a newer, more angular, design will also be available soon. A kit for a fine model of a GWR Steam Railmotor is produced in 4 mm scale (and also in 7 mm scale) by Mallard Models.

For a modern branch line layout Modern Traction Kits (MTK) offer a range of Diesel Multiple Units. Various diesel locomotives have been used for passenger and freight services

A Grafar GWR 0-6-0 Class 9410 Pannier Tank Engine, also available in BR livery.

Locomotives and rolling stock

Above An Airfix 6110 Class GWR 2-6-2 Prairie Tank. Below A Lima Class 45XX Small Prairie Tank, seen here in GWR colours but also produced in BR lined black livery Bottom A Wrenn SR Class R1 0-6-0 Tank. Above right Langley Miniature Models produce a white metal kit for the Great Western Railway streamlined diesel railcar in N scale designed to fit onto a Lifelike diesel chassis. This picture shows the completed model (Photograph by courtesy of Langley Miniature Models.) Right A Wills Finecast 2-4-0 'Metro' Tank. This cast metal kit model can be built as the open cab version as shown here or with a closed cab. (Photograph by courtesy of Wills.)

on branch lines. Modern Traction Kits and Q Kits both produce ranges of diesel locomotive kits in 4 mm scale. For goods services on some branches BR Class 08 shunters have been employed; in 00 a ready-to-run model is made by Wrenn and there is a kit manufactured by Modern Traction Kits.

In N scale the range is more limited but Grafar have ready-to-run models of the GWR and BR Class 94XX Pannier Tank, a Prairie Tank in GWR and BR livery, and 0-6-0 Tank Engines for other railway companies. There is a steadily increasing selection of cast metal kits designed to fit onto various commercially produced chassis. Langley Miniature Models, for example, have recently introduced a cast metal and etched brass kit for a GWR 14XX 0-4-2 Tank Locomotive and Autocoach. This firm also makes kits for the GWR streamlined diesel railcar and twin railcars designed to fit onto Lifelike GP 40 chassis. The carriages used on local passenger trains on branch lines were often older mainline stock passed down to the minor lines, though the GWR also used auto-coaches and 'B' sets. Through trains were usually made up of corridor coaches. A good range of ready-to-run and kit models are available, particularly in 00 scale.

Goods traffic was mainly carried in open wagons and in vans, with coal and foodstuffs forming the bulk of the traffic, though the transport of livestock, especially cattle, was also of some importance. Special stock will need some reason for its presence, for example, an appropriate industry on the line. There is an excellent range of wagons and vans both ready-to-run and kit models in 00 and a lesser but adequate selection in N.

Generally, the selection of locomotives, coaches and goods stock is good and is improving all the time so that the enthusiast should have no problem in providing adequate stock for a branch line layout, certainly in the two most popular scales.

Locomotives and rolling stock

Structures and scenery

More general information on structure model-ling is provided in another book in this series, *PSL Model Railway Guide 3, Structure Modelling,* but there are a few relevant comments which I would like to make here. At branch line stations the structures are, or were, usually fairly small and simple and there were relatively few of them at a typical small terminus. All these features are advantageous for the beginner working in a small area.

The station buildings would include a booking office and a parcels office, a waiting room, toilets, a staff room and a lamp room as basic features at a small station. At larger terminii more facilities would be provided. If it was necessary for passengers to cross from one platform to another there might be a footbridge though often the passengers would use a barrow crossing. Other structures usually present include a goods shed, an engine shed and a signal box.

For the initial construction of the layout the modeller can utilise kits from the excellent ranges available. These include the accurate models of specific prototypes produced as full colour card kits by Prototype Models; many of these are replicas of branch line structures and are ideal for a layout of this type. The Super-quick, Bilteezi and Builder Plus ranges also include a number of buildings suitable for branch line layouts. Plastic kit models are offered by Airfix, Malvern Models and Peco, while Hornby make a selection of colour printed, plastic, clip-together structure kits for 00 scale. Grafar have a range of ready made structure models in N scale.

Later the modeller may wish to replace some or all of the kit built models by scratch-built models to provide greater authenticity for a model of a specific branch, or to give more individuality, or to enable the modeller to include replicas of prototype buildings he particularly likes.

Information about buildings on specific branch lines may be available in books on these railways, and in some cases scale drawings are included. Two excellent books of this type are *Great Western Branch Line Termini,* Vols 1 & 2, by Paul Karau, and a fine model of Walling-ford station inspired by Vol 1, built by Iain C. Robinson was described in the November 1979 issue of *Railway Modeller* magazine. This article gives a full description of the methods used by Mr Robinson to scratch-build these structures, methods which will be just as useful for other buildings, and I recommend it to would be scratch builders. Another useful book, also from the Oxford Publishing Company, is *Great Western Architecture,* a very comprehensive survey of GWR buildings.

Other books providing drawings of attractive structure models suitable for branch line layouts, both railway buildings and lineside structures, together with useful information on construction include John Ahern's *Miniature Building Construction* published by Argus, and *Downesplans Book 2 Railway Buildings,* by Allan Downes, published by Peco. Platform details and other accessories are available as plastic or white metal models from Mikes Models, Dart Castings, Airfix, John Piper (accessories) Ltd, Ratio and other manufacturers.

Above right *Prototype Models make a range of colour printed card structure kits in 2 mm, 4 mm and 7 mm scales. These attractive models are accurate replicas of actual railway buildings and many are ideal for branch line layouts. The selection of 4 mm scale models shown here includes from left to right: Chalford Goods Office, Standard GWR Signal Box, Wilmcote Station Shelter, Tetbury Engine Shed and Chalford Station, all from the Great Western.* (Photograph by courtesy of Prototype Models.)

Right *The station buildings at 'Stonepark Lane', an 00-scale branch line terminus, were constructed from a Superquick kit. Despite its impressive appearance the structure measures only 9 inches by 7½ inches.*

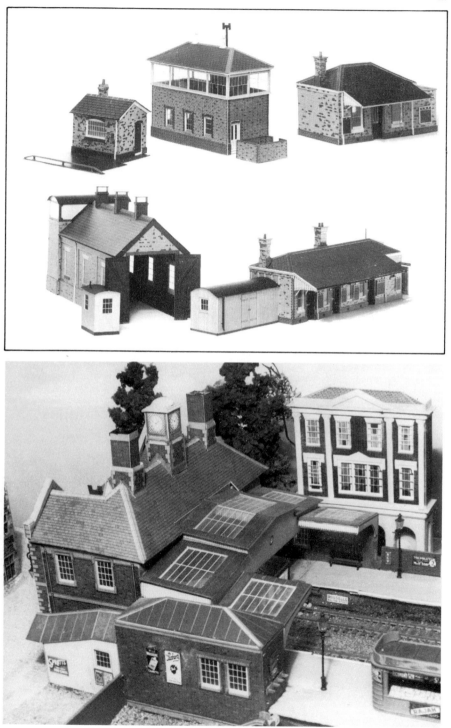

Structures and scenery

The modelling of scenery for model railway layouts is also covered in another book in this series, *PSL Model Railway Guide 4, Scenery.* The scenic work is important on a branch line layout because one of the essential features of this type of model is that it should be realistic. This can only be achieved if the setting is modelled with as much care and attention to detail as the railway itself. Initially, in an effort to get the layout complete enough for operation fairly quickly, the modeller may prefer to keep the scenic work basic and simple. Later

The structures on the Watlington Branch layout, including this beautifully detailed station building, were scratch-built by Barry Fisher. All are accurate replicas of the prototype railway buildings.

more detail can be added and, as the layout will be relatively small, there is no reason why the scenery should not be brought to quite a high standard of detail and realism without too much work being required.

Operation

One of the advantages of branch line modelling is that the resulting layout can be operated in a realistic and authentic manner. Thus instead of merely running trains around at random we have a proper pattern of operation and this makes the layout much more interesting to use. If you model a particular prototype exactly you may wish to follow the working timetable for the branch concerned. Though these were originally issued only to employees, many have now been published. For example, the books *Great Western Branch Line Termini* Vols 1 & 2 contain the working timetables for the branches described. Alternatively, some research may be necessary to obtain details for the line you are modelling. If you adapt a prototype or have created your own station from various features from different prototypes you can either use a prototype timetable or can devise your own.

Prototype timetables are often rather limited and operation following one may not be of great interest so it may be preferable to make up your own to suit. When following a timetable there are two main schemes of operation. The first method is to run the trains according to time. Since a branch line timetable will have long pauses between trains when nothing is happening it is necessary to use a speeded up time system with an hour on the timetable represented by five or ten minutes of actual time. Often a clock in which the gearing has been altered to produce this speeding up is employed, or more simply movements of the minute hand are read off so that five minutes or ten minutes on the clock are taken to represent an hour. In fact this system is at its best on a larger layout where there is more than one operator and the time on the clock then provides a constant factor to which all the operators work. By reference to the clock, train movements are carried out in the correct order, trains meet and pass at the right times and places, and so on. Thus orderly operation can be achieved.

On a small layout, where there is often only one operator, much of this is irrelevant and unnecessary and the second method is more suitable. Here the operator works to the timetable sequence but ignores the actual time. Once a particular movement has been carried out he goes on to the next in the sequence. Thus train movements are carried out in the correct order and the pattern of running is maintained.

It is quite easy to develop a timetable for your own branch line terminus starting with a few trains, passenger and goods, and adding more as you buy or build more locomotives and rolling stock. At first just develop a single day's operation, arranging it so that after you have worked the timetable sequence through the trains will be back in their original positions ready for the next session. Later you can devise different timetables for other days such as Wednesday (market day) Saturday and Sunday. As you become more experienced you can add extra trains, unscheduled specials, maintenance of way trains, and so on. Additional interest can be supplied by an occasional breakdown or derailment which will cause delays and changes to the schedule. However it is best to let your timetable develop as you go along rather than trying to devise a complicated scheme from the very start.

Generally in planning the layout and its operation we want as many train movements as possible at the station to keep up the interest in operation. Thus it is usually better, for example, to run a passenger train of two or three coaches round which the engine must run to reverse the train, rather than an auto-train or railcar which merely runs back in reverse, though these can be included in the timetable to add variety. Similarly we need as many different facilities as possible at the station to increase the variety of rolling stock and the amount of shunting needed when goods trains arrive. The subject of operation is dealt with in detail in another book in this series, *PSL Model Railway Guide 5, Operating Your Layout.*

Further developments

Earlier I mentioned that while it is convenient for the beginner that a branch line layout could be brought to a fairly complete state reasonably quickly, this can also be a disadvantage as the modeller may then find he loses interest because the scope for any further construction appears very limited. In this section I want to explore some of the possibilities for extending the interest.

The enthusiast who enjoys scratch-building and super-detailing may like to gradually replace all the structures, perhaps originally simple kit models, by highly detailed hand-built models, perhaps based on actual prototype structures. If internal lighting and interior detailing are also provided the construction work can be extended even further. Similarly there are many opportunities for fine detailing with the addition of lamps, seats, barrows and other accessories of appropriate company style and period to the platforms and station areas. Human and animal figures are available commercially both as plastic and as cast metal models. The former may be painted or

unpainted when purchased, the latter are only available unpainted. Careful painting, and in some cases additions or alterations to clothing, tools held in the hands, and so on, can improve and individualise the models.

Many trackside details can be added to give a more realistic and authentic appearance. Some of the accompanying photographs show such details on the Watlington Branch layout built by members of the Mid Hants Model Railway Group. The point rodding, made up from etched brass parts manufactured by Colin Waite, is particularly effective. Such detailing is fiddly to add but can keep the modeller amused for some time and the results are worth while as the finished appearance is most realistic. In the same way the scenery beyond the tracks can be systematically brought up to a very high standard of detail. Individual plants of recognisable varieties can be modelled as has been done on the magnificent dioramas in the Pendon Museum.

All this additional construction work can be carried on without interrupting operations on the layout. Further improvements can be the provision of realistic road vehicles, lorries, vans, cars, buses, motorcycles and bicycles of appropriate period, either made up from commercial kits or scratch-built. Further scope for construction lies in the replacement of the ready-to-run locomotives and rolling stock employed to get the layout into operation fairly quickly by kit or scratch-built models. Alternatively you may wish to retain your original

Very realistic track detailing on the EM gauge Watlington Branch layout built by the Mid Hants Model Railway Group. **Left** *Sleepers form this simple block across the rails preventing stock from running off the end of the track.* **Above right** *Though the points are operated electrically with point motors beneath the baseboard, dummy point levers have been added for authenticity.* **Above far right** *The beautifully modelled point rodding made up from Colin Waite parts gives a complete appearance to the track area.*

roster but add to it slowly by building extra models.

An interesting way of increasing the potential of a limited layout is to provide locomotives, rolling stock and accessories for two distinct and different periods, for example pre- and post-grouping. In many cases structures have survived relatively unchanged for many years so the basic track layout, structures and scenery can serve both periods. By changing the locomotives and rolling stock, and accessories such as motor vehicles and human figures (because of the changes in fashions of dress) we can represent different periods on the layout. Thus we can provide scope for additional locomotive and rolling stock construction as well as giving variety in appearance when operating the layout. For their Watlington Branch exhibition layout the Mid Hants Model Railway Group have locomotives and rolling stock for both pre-grouping and post-grouping periods and this has made the layout more interesting, both for them to operate and for the public to view.

All the above suggestions have been made on the assumption that no extension of the layout is possible. However, it may well be that additional sections can be constructed, even if they must be portable units to be stored away when not actually in use, to fit onto the original layout. The terminus to fiddle yard type of layout is particularly suitable for this as extra sections can be made, as convenient to the modeller, and when complete can be fitted between the original sections. These additional units may be purely scenic or can include a through station or a halt to add interest to the timetable operation. If more space becomes available you may even be able to model the junction station. Eventually the branch line may become merely part of a larger layout.

Another idea which can be considered is the modelling of a narrow-gauge feeder line as an addition to your branch line model. A prototype example is the Swanage Branch with exchange sidings at Furzebrook and at Eldon Sidings where clay was transferred from the narrow-gauge lines from the clay pits of Purbeck. Another alternative would be a narrow-gauge feeder from a stone quarry or a mine. Such a line could be fitted into a relatively small space but will add greatly to the operational possibilities as well as being very attractive scenically.

Other types of branches

Modern

Though the original concept of branch line modelling referred essentially to the steam worked lines in a period up to the 1950s, a number of branch lines have survived and are still in operation today. There have, however, been considerable changes with the introduction of diesel or electric motive power and with the various modifications designed to improve cost effectiveness by modernisation and automation. Track layouts have been simplified by removing tracks no longer necessary with the cessation of goods traffic and with no need for run-around facilities for the diesel or electric units employed for passenger traffic. Station buildings have been altered, though many original structures can still be seen. Some buildings have been demolished to save on repairs, painting and rates payments. Small stations are unmanned with tickets sold on the train or at the larger stations. Colour light signalling has in many cases replaced the semaphore signals previously present and barrier crossings or train operated unguarded level crossings have taken over from the old gated crossings. Though there have been so many changes there are still many features which will make these lines interesting in model form. There is also the great advantage of being able to directly observe the prototype which is being modelled thus ensuring accuracy and an authentic atmosphere. The biggest drawback is the very limited operational scope most of these branches now offer, often little more than a DMU shuttling back and forth, with no opportunities for shunting.

However, some branches do offer rather more interesting operation and a good case is made by J.G. Glover in the September 1979 issue of *Railway Modeller* magazine for Bourne End station as the basis of a modern branch line layout. The article and accompanying track plan are well worth consideration if you are interested in the idea of modelling a present day line. Suitable rolling stock is available in kit form in both 00 and N from Modern Traction

Kits, who offer a good range of DMUs. The modeller who likes DMUs would find such a branch an ideal setting for an interesting selection of kit built models. Later, if desired, it could be incorporated into a larger layout, perhaps a main line scheme, as a branch from it.

Modern goods and industrial branches can still offer interesting and busy operation and later in this book I want to look at a goods branch serving a dock and industrial area in Poole which would make a good basis for a layout. The other modern period branch line we can consider modelling is the preserved line.

Preserved

For the modeller who likes, and has perhaps already collected, a wide variety of loco- motives, a selection which would not normally be seen together because of their origins, period or type, a very attractive solution can be to model a preserved line. One can then even include some foreign engines if they take your fancy as there are several prototype precedents for this! For example, the Nene Valley Railway has locomotives from Denmark, Sweden and France, as well as continental rolling stock including Danish and Norwegian coaches, while the Kent & East Sussex Railway roster of locomotives includes an American Tank and a Norwegian State 2-6-0 Tender Engine.

You might like to base your layout on an actual preserved line. This has the advantage that you can visit the branch to see and photo- graph everything and there is often plenty of published data about the locomotives, rolling stock, stations and so on. The model could be a representation of the line as it is now, or as the preservation society hope to make it. Such a model could be very satisfying and could also have considerable publicity value for the rail- way. Providing locomotive and rolling stock models for most lines should not be a problem using the standard commercial products.

Another approach would be to model a branch line you like which has been closed, as though it had been preserved. This will give you more freedom in the design of the layout and in the choice of locomotives and rolling stock than if you were modelling an actual preserved line. A third alternative is to model an entirely imaginary preserved line of your own design.

There are many interesting details which can be added to a layout representing a preserved branch line. There may be locomotives and rolling stock awaiting or undergoing repairs, some scrapped items kept to provide spare parts for other equipment, many parts lying around, and perhaps numerous visitors, many with cameras taking pictures! Often equipment not normally seen on a branch line, such as a heavy breakdown crane, has been acquired by preserved lines and is to be seen at the station or in the workshop area. There may also be a small museum of other items such as traction engines, vintage cars or buses and so on. If you model a station on the preserved line as one combined with British Rail then you have the perfect excuse for including everything from vintage steam engines on the preserved line to the High Speed Train on the BR tracks! All on the one layout!

Foreign

Just as the branch line layout concept was essentially related to the steam period it was also really applied to British prototypes, especially the Great Western Railway branch lines. However, there does seem to be an increasing interest in modelling foreign railways, usually American or European. This, I think, is partly due to increasing familiarity with

these prototypes through holidays abroad and the availability of information in both British and foreign railway and model railway books and magazines. The importation of models of foreign locomotives and rolling stock, and of kits for structures, mostly of excellent quality, also has a significant influence. Thus the popularity of modelling German railways must surely be related to the excellence both in variety and in quality of the range of models available in various scales, particularly HO and N.

There has at times been criticism in the British model railway press of foreign prototype layouts, especially German based lines, built by British modellers. In many cases the models appear unrealistic because the modeller is insufficiently familiar with the prototype, its setting and its methods of operation. Now if the enthusiast is happy with his layout and derives enjoyment and pleasure from it then its inaccuracies are unimportant. This is, after all, a hobby and it is up to the individual how he builds and operates his layout. However, most modellers will find that a realistic and authentic layout based accurately on the appearances and practices of the prototype will give the most satisfaction. To achieve this it is important to familiarise yourself with everything about the prototype

Useful details for modellers at Shackerstone Station, once a branch line junction station on the Midland Railway and now preserved, include a gas lamp, an MR boundary marker and the advertisements.

and its setting. Operating practice and track layout is often rather different from the British system and this should be taken into account when designing a layout.

For American modelling the range of ready-to-run models, kits and parts in HO and N scales is excellent and the enthusiast can obtain a great deal of information about modelling American branch and short line railroads from reading one or more of the fine model railroad magazines produced in the United States.

The range of European models in HO and N scales is also very good though the emphasis is almost entirely on ready-to-run equipment; this is generally of excellent quality. Some countries, particularly Germany, France and Switzerland, are very well catered for by the manufacturers but for others there is much less available. There is a good deal of prototype information available, in English, for the modeller, and several countries have model railway magazines, though here there may be language problems, of course. Ideally one should visit the country concerned and take as many photographs as possible to guide you in the modelling of the setting, the trackside details, and so on, in addition to the more obviously important locomotives, rolling stock and railway buildings.

For other countries of the world much converting or scratch building will be required to complete a layout and such a project is only really suitable for the more experienced modeller with a particular interest in, and knowledge of, the railway system concerned.

Research

I have already commented on the value of general background reading to the branch line modeller in giving some idea of the character and appearance of the prototype lines. If you are planning to base your layout on a particular station, or on several stations selecting the features you like from each and combining them, then more specific information will be required. The research involved in obtaining this will not only be invaluable in the construction of a realistic model but can also be very interesting and enjoyable in itself.

At the time when branch line modelling was first put forward as a good choice there were many branch lines still operating and they were still using steam locomotives. Thus if one of these lines was chosen as the prototype to be followed, simply visiting the railway would enable the modeller to obtain and record all the information needed. Now most of the branches have closed and those which have survived have often been considerably modified. If the enthusiast wishes to model a line which is still in use, as it is today, then there is, of course, no problem as a visit to the line with camera and notebook will give him all the data required. It is particularly convenient if the line is fairly local to the modeller's home so that return visits can be easily made as necessary to obtain further information or to check on details which have been previously overlooked. This is a point worth considering in the choice of prototype. You may want to model a branch which is still in operation as it was at an earlier period, perhaps in the later days of steam. Even though there will probably have been changes in the track layout, structures, and so on, much valuable information can still be obtained from visits. This data will be a useful basis to which you can add as you refer to books, photographs and maps describing and illustrating what the line was like before the recent modernisation.

Even on lines which have been closed, perhaps for many years, it is worth while visiting the site if you can. Though the tracks have been lifted you can often still see the line of the track and the type of scenic setting. Some structures may still be there and even though these may be in very poor condition the basic dimensions can still be accurately measured. Sometimes you will find that old station buildings have been converted into private houses and again, despite the alterations, it may be possible to obtain useful measurements. Remember that closed lines are now usually privately owned land and buildings and that you have no automatic right of access no matter how worth while you feel your research is. However, a polite request and explanation of why you want to view the site will usually meet with co-operation from the owner.

An alternative source of prototype information is from published work. Though the present day modeller is at a disadvantage compared to the enthusiast in the 1950s when it comes to viewing the prototype, he has a much greater range of published data available to him. A very great deal of information regarding branch lines has appeared in print, with more coming out all the time and, if the line you wish to model has been covered, much of your research may already have been done for you.

The model railway magazines have featured many prototype branch lines over the years, with descriptions, photographs, usually track plans and, often, suggestions on modelling. Because the articles are generally slanted towards the modeller they are particularly helpful in providing the information he requires. Back issues of model railway magazines are often to be found in second-hand book shops, and specialist booksellers, such as Lens of Sutton, hold extensive stocks of back numbers. The prototype railway magazines have also featured many useful and informative articles on branch lines and again back issues can be obtained from second-hand and specialist booksellers. Many model railway clubs have collections of magazines in their libraries which are available to members. Alternatively you may find that members have

The track has been lifted on this branch line in Northumberland but the signal cabin remains. Though there is minor damage the structure is essentially intact enabling the modeller to obtain accurate measurements.

suitable for the modeller, and even working timetables. This firm also offers pictorial albums on Great Western, Scottish, LNER and Southern branch lines. Recently published by Wild Swan Publications (WSP) is *Branch Lines of the Southern Railway* by George Reeve & Chris Hawkins which provides excellent coverage of four Southern branches, including Swanage and Hayling. There are also useful books on specific aspects of railways which can be very helpful in modelling. For example *A Pictorial Record of Great Western Signalling* by A. Vaughan and *A Pictorial Record of Southern Signals* by G. Pryer, both published by OPC.

You may be able to obtain details of the track layout of the prototype in which you are interested from one of these books or from magazine article coverage. Alternatively many station plans are available through the BR/OPC Joint Venture (302 Holdenhurst Road, Bournemouth). An extensive range of GWR station track plans is already available with SR stations to follow shortly. Under this arrangement between British Rail and the Oxford Publishing Company many plans of structures, locomotives, rolling stock, etc and a wide range of photographs are also available to the modeller.

If the station or branch in which you are interested is not covered in this way Ordnance Survey maps will provide details in many cases. The large scale maps are needed for this purpose and may be available at libraries in the area concerned. Photographs of the station or branch can be invaluable in the creation of a realistic model and there are a number of firms specialising in railway photographs. I have already mentioned the BR/OPC Joint Venture. Lens of Sutton also have an excellent range, while Aerofilms of Boreham Wood have many photographs of stations, both period and modern, from the air which may be useful in planning your layout and in modelling the scenery.

personal collections of magazines which include the issues to which you want to refer.

Various categories of books are available on the subject of branch lines. I have already mentioned those offering a more general coverage, with three examples. A second type of book is the photographic album or pictorial book. These again usually give a fairly general coverage, though this time in pictures, often of branch lines in one area or region. These books are useful for background, atmosphere and, in some cases, from the scenic modelling aspect.

There is also a steadily increasing number of detailed books on particular branch lines or stations and these are invaluable if your chosen prototype is covered. The Oakwood Press have an extensive list of railway titles, a number of which are on branch lines. The Oxford Railway Publishing Company Ltd (OPC) have published a series of Branch Line Histories and there are further titles planned. Two excellent books from this publisher are *Great Western Branch Line Termini* (Vol 1) and (Vol 2) both by Paul Karau. The first covers Fairford, Lambourn, Tetbury, Wallingford, and Watlington, while the second features Abbotsbury, Ashburton, Hemyock, Moretonhampstead and Princetown. The surveys of the stations are very detailed with many photographs and drawings

Layouts

Having taken a fairly general look at the idea of branch line modelling I would now like to show you a few examples in various popular scales, though I would emphasise that 00 scale is really the ideal choice for the beginner. The layouts vary considerably in size and while two are closely based on particular prototype branches the others are not modelled on any specific lines though they do follow the general practices of the prototype.

Stonepark Lane

This L-shaped branch line terminus to fiddle yard 00-gauge layout is an example of what can be achieved using mainly commercially available items, in some cases modified to suit the situation. Much of the construction work was carried out by Paul Holmes who originally owned the layout but some modifications have been made by Ralph Fenwick, the present owner, who also plans to extend the layout when more space becomes available. The track layout is simple and only six points have been used, four at the terminus and two in the fiddle yard, which represents the junction with the main line at the other end of the branch.

The main section of the layout is L shaped and rests permanently on bookcases in the corner of the room. Two additional sections are temporarily fixed onto this for operating sessions. A simple fiddle yard with two points leading to three sidings fits on beyond the beach while a narrow strip of chipboard with a single track is positioned at the station end of the layout to make shunting of the goods siding more convenient. Later it is hoped to expand this to include some industrial sidings or a small harbour.

The baseboards are pieces of three-quarter inch thick chipboard and, as they are fitted onto the top of bookcases, bracing was not needed for further strengthening. Track and

Stonepark Lane is an 00-gauge branch line terminus constructed by Paul Holmes. Most of the buildings are based on commercially produced kits.

turnouts are Peco, mostly laid on foam underlay. Additional ballast and careful painting of the underlay and the sides of the rails has given a very realistic appearance and the foam makes the track very smooth and free running. The points near the level crossing are hand operated but the others at the terminus are moved by Peco point motors concealed by buildings or scenery. The points in the fiddle yard are operated by Hammant & Morgan point motors. The buffers are from Peco kits.

The station buildings were assembled from the Superquick Terminus station kit while the platforms were built up from thick card. The goods shed is a modified Superquick kit. The low relief structures at the rear give the impression of a road behind the station with houses and shops along it. Though they occupy very little space they complete the scene very effectively. The small hill, through which the line passes in a cutting and a short

Low relief structures

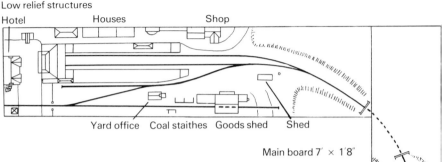

Hotel   Houses   Shop

Yard office   Coal staithes Goods shed   Shed

Main board 7′ × 1′8″
Smaller board 4′ × 1′4″

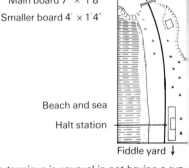

Beach and sea

Halt station

Fiddle yard ↓

Above *Track plan for Stonepark Lane, an 00-gauge branch line terminus.*

Below *An Airfix Private Owner wagon awaits collection after emptying. Note the coal staithes made from old sleepers.*

Above right *The parcels depot is from the Superquick Terminus Station kit. The porter and milk churns are Merit products and the GWR Siphon F van was built from a K's kit.*

tunnel, has a basis of chunks of polystyrene foam supporting chicken wire netting. Over this is a covering of Mod-Roc and plaster, painted appropriately and with suitably coloured scenis dressings applied over it. The sea is ripple glass over painted hardboard.

The layout is operated as a Great Western branch using a simple timetable. The locomotives now include a Hornby 0-6-0 Pannier Tank, a Lima Small Prairie and Airfix 14XX Class 0-4-2 and Prairie Tanks. A Lima GWR diesel railcar will be added to the roster as soon as it is on the market. Coaches include four Triang clerestories, one of which is a brake end, an Airfix autocoach and a BSL kit built autocoach. Goods stock is from various ready-to-run ranges, together with a K's kit built GWR Siphon van. A Hornby light crane forms part of an engineers department train used for maintenance of way and for derailments.

The terminus is unusual in not having a run-around loop and a release cross-over could have been included on the two main platform roads, making operation more convenient. However, an isolated section has been provided at the end of each of these tracks so that another engine can be used to pull the train out and release the original engine. This is not necessary for the push-pull trains.

Stonepark Lane illustrates how an interesting and attractive branch line layout can be built in relatively little space and at low cost. Even though most items on the layout are readily available commercial products, the resulting model is realistic and individual.

The Sherrington branch

Sherrington is a typical branch line terminus model of the type so popular in 00 gauge but the choice of N gauge has meant that only a

Below and bottom *Two views of Sherrington Station, an N-scale branch line terminus. Most of the structures on this layout were scratch-built. The excellent scenic work has created a very realistic overall appearance.*

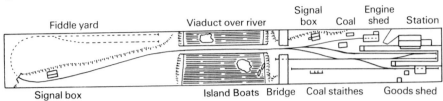

Fiddle yard | Viaduct over river | Signal box | Coal | Engine shed | Station

Signal box | Island Boats | Bridge | Coal staithes | Goods shed

Layout 10'4" long 1'3" wide

Track plan for the N-scale Sherrington Branch.

minimum of space has been necessary for an interesting layout. The terminus section measures only 4 feet by 15 inches and the fiddle yard section is identical in size. A linking section 28 inches by 15 inches completes the layout, the overall dimensions of which are thus 10 feet 4 inches by 15 inches. Because such small radius curves can be employed in N gauge a 180 degree turn has been possible on the 15-inch wide baseboard to reach the fiddle yard sidings. Thus this section of the layout provides a full length of visible line and scenery as well as accommodating the hidden sidings.

Sherrington was originally owned by J.

Harvey Watkins who carried out most of the construction work on the station section. He later sold the layout to Eric Kay who developed it further adding the river section with its impressive viaduct. Baseboard construction follows conventional methods with a wood fibre insulation board top supported by wood framing. The three sections bolt together and the detachable wooden legs are also bolted into position. When not in use the layout is easily taken apart into small units which can be stored or transported without difficulty. The track and points are all Peco with all the points controlled by Peco point motors mounted

A Grafar GWR Prairie Tank on shed at Sherrington. The typical water tower and coaling stage were scratch-built from card and plastic.

เeath the baseboard top. The track was
ed directly down onto the insulation board
I ballasted with granite dust giving a very
listic appearance. Landscaping was carried
t with plaster bandage material and Polyfilla
ile the rock faces are made from cork. After
nting the scenery surface various scenic
ssings were sprinkled on to give the
oearance of grass, earth, and so on. The
er was painted appropriately and then given
oat of gloss varnish to produce a wet look.
All of the structures at the terminus, with the
ception of the station building — a modified
la kit, were scratch-built. Construction was
m plastic card, commercial brick and slate
oers and stone embossed plastic sheet. The
je viaduct over the river was modelled from
ystyrene foam carved to give the effect of
network. Many small details such as signs,
nals and telegraph poles, scratch-built from
ds and ends, add to the overall effect of the
idel. Locomotives and rolling stock are
dy-to-run models from various ranges
iropriate to a Great Western branch in the
er days of steam. The layout is operated to
ietable and when two operators are available
imple bell code can be employed between
i station and fiddle yard. The layout has

been shown at a number of exhibitions very
successfully.

The Swanage branch

This 00-gauge model railway shows that a
branch line layout need not be small and
simple! The prototype Swanage line, opened in
1885, branched from the main Wareham-
Dorchester route at Wogret Junction and then
ran nearly ten miles to Swanage. The only
intermediate station was at Corfe Castle,
approximately half way along the branch. The
line was an important one and in the busy
holiday periods each summer there were many
long distance trains arriving at Swanage, with
through trains from as far afield as the
Midlands and the North. Freight was also
important, particularly the traffic in clay. The
branch was operated by steam until 1967 when
diesel units took over and carried on the local
services. The line was closed in 1972 except for
the short section from Wogret Junction to
Furzebrook which has remained in operation
for the bulk freight traffic in clay and oil. The
Swanage Railway Society was formed in 1972
with the aim of reopening the branch and trains

ck plan for the EM-gauge Watlington Branch constructed by members of the Mid Hants Model
ilway Group.

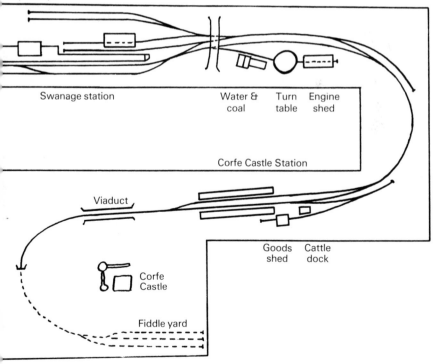

Swanage station

Water &
coal

Turn
table

Engine
shed

Corfe Castle Station

Viaduct

Goods
shed

Cattle
dock

Corfe
Castle

Fiddle yard

are run over a short length of track at Swanage at weekends.

The 00-gauge model was constructed some years ago by Terry Jenkins and other members of the Isle of Purbeck Model Railway Club as an exhibition and club layout. The aim was to reproduce the appearance and atmosphere of the real line as accurately as possible within the limitations imposed by space and finance. The layout of the stations at Swanage and Corfe Castle has been based quite closely on the prototype but naturally the line between has been markedly compressed. Even so the model requires a large room to accommodate it.

Baseboard construction was heavier than usual on home layouts to withstand the harder

usage of exhibition halls and club room b otherwise followed the usual methods. Tra and points were entirely hand built to redu expense. The scenery was built up from plas bandage material and plaster, painted and th covered with scenic dressings. Lichen v used extensively for bushes, hedges and tre though some Britains trees were also includ on the layout. An interesting method construction was developed for the sto railway and other buildings on the moc including the accurate replica of the ruir Corfe Castle which is a major scenic feature the layout. Over a basis of thick card a layer Pyruma (Kos) fire cement was applied a scribed to represent the individual stones of

Left *Corfe Castle station on the 00-scale Swangage Branch layout built by Terry Jenkins and other members of the Isle of Purbeck Model Railway Club. The station buildings and goods shed were scratch-built with stonework modelled by scribing Pyruma fire cement.*

Below left *Swanage water tower and coaling stage scratch-built in 4 mm scale.*

Above *As a Triang 0-4-4 M7 Class Tank locomotive arrives at Swanage with a goods train a Hornby 0-6-0 Tank is about to run off the turntable into the engine shed.*

Right *The ruins of Corfe Castle realistically modelled in 4 mm scale for the Swanage Branch layout.*

buildings. The cement was then allowed to harden and the resulting effect was very good.

Locomotives and rolling stock used on the line belonged to various club members. Most were ready-to-run models though many have been repainted or modified. The basis of the locomotive roster were Triang M7 0-4-4 Tanks and a variety of 0-6-0 Tank Engines, though larger locomotives were also run on through trains. Timetable operation following the original prototype working timetables could be carried out but at shows more intensive running was often provided to maintain interest for the spectators. A change in clubrooms necessitated the sale of the layout some time ago.

The Watlington Branch

The Watlington Branch has been one of my favourite lines ever since I first came across the descriptions of Watlington and Aston Rowant stations by John Ahern in *Model Railway News* back in August and September 1950, so I was delighted to see this model by the Mid Hants Model Railway Group at a recent exhibition. The layout, in EM gauge, is based very accurately on Watlington station and gives a realistic picture of how this terminus must have appeared.

The prototype branch from Princes Risborough to Watlington was opened in 1872 by the Watlington & Princes Risborough Railway Company but it was taken over in 1883 by the Great Western. The line was operated on the 'One Engine in Steam' principle, the locomotive being shedded at Watlington overnight. The working timetable consisted of Up and Down goods trains in the morning and evening, with passenger trains during the day.

The model features the end of the line from Lewknor Halt to Watlington and the layout is

Layouts

A general view of the approach to Watlington Station on the EM gauge layout constructed by th Mid Hants Model Railway Group. The EM gauge track and the overall high standard of th modelling have created a very realistic appearance. Note the nail in hinge method of joining th baseboard sections, visible in the foreground on the right. The bell at the rear is used f communication between fiddle yard and terminus operators when timetable running is progress.

18 feet 6 inches long, including the fiddle yard, which is of an interesting design with four sidings on a large sector plate. The Group plans to extend the distance between Watlington and Lewknor Halt stations and later it is hoped to incorporate the layout as a branch line terminus on another layout which is at present under construction.

The baseboards are of the solid top with supporting framing type and have detachable legs; the layout can be transported to exhibitions in two cars or in a small van. Track and points were hand-built using EM Gauge Society components, with SMP track employed on the sector table in the fiddle yard. All points are controlled by Hammant &

Morgan motors fitted beneath the baseboa top, but dummy hand levers are also include on the model for realism. Locomotive control by linked section using Scalespeed controllers

The beautifully detailed structure mode were made from plastic card and are accura replicas of the real buildings on the branch. Th scenery was shaped from polystyrene foa covered with plaster and given a realist texture while trees were modelled with wi trunks and branches and foliage of scourin pads. Many small details including telegra poles, fences and signs have been accurate modelled and there are numerous figures appropriate period dress. Most of the figur are detachable for storage and are fixed

A view of Lewknor Bridge Halt on the Watlington Branch. The structure was scratch-built. T gas lamps are from the Mike's Models range of cast metal accessories.

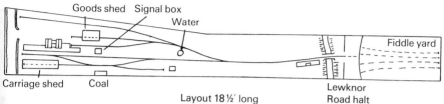

Goods shed   Signal box
Water
Fiddle yard
Carriage shed   Coal
Lewknor
Road halt

Layout 18½′ long

The Swanage Branch as modelled by the Isle of Purbeck MRC. (Not to scale.)

place on the layout by means of a wire attached beneath one foot which fits into a hole in the baseboard surface.

At exhibitions the layout can be operated using two sequence tables, one based on the Working Timetable of the 1920s/30s, the other an expanded version to show visitors a wider display of rolling stock and requiring more than one locomotive at Watlington. Most of the locomotives used on the layout were constructed from white metal and etched brass kits, with added details, and a few were scratch-built. Most of the locomotives are fitted with Mike Sharman wheels. Coaches are ready-to-run models suitably modified, mainly Triang clerestories, or from Ratio Coach parts cut and spliced together appropriately. The goods stock is from kits, mainly Slater's and Ratio, together with some scratch-built items. An interesting feature is the provision of locomotives and rolling stock for two distinct periods, pre- and post-grouping, adding to the variety and hence to the appeal of the layout. Regrettably, Barry Fisher who was the instigator of this layout and who built the structures, died suddenly in January 1979.

The Fort Ness Branch

This N-scale layout built by Alan Copas is an interesting example of a continuous oval track design with part of the oval concealed and provided with sidings to form a fiddle yard. The visible part of the layout features Fort Ness, a small through station between Inverness and Glasgow. When the branch to Fort William is constructed it will lead off from the front right-hand side of the layout and Fort Ness will become a junction station. In the meantime the arrangement of hidden tracks within the dotted line and the rear of the backscene forms a mock-up of the intended track plan for Fort William, enabling Alan to try out the design in advance.

The period of the layout is set at the time of the transition from steam to diesel to that both forms of motive power can be represented. Locomotives and rolling stock are mainly ready-to-run models from various manufacturers. Operation as a through station and junction allows Alan to justifiably run larger locomotives and longer trains than on a branch.

Track plan of the Fort Ness N-scale layout constructed by Alan Copas.

Section within dotted lines is a mock-up of future Fort William track plan

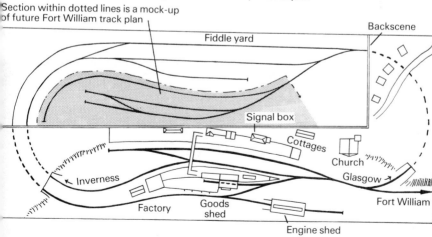

Backscene

Fiddle yard

Signal box

Cottages

Church

Inverness

Glasgow

Fort William

Factory   Goods
shed

Engine shed

Layouts

Above *A through passenger train made up of Minitrix coaches hauled by a Minitrix British Ra* *Type 2 diesel at Fort Ness on the N-scale layout constructed by Alan Copas. The main statio building was made up from a Hambling's Bilteezi card kit. The attractive backscene has bee assembled from pictures cut from calendars.*

Below *The goods shed at Fort Ness was built by Alan Copas from a Highfield card kit while th canopy behind it is from a Pola kit. The footbridge in the left background is an old Lone Sta model.*

Bottom *This J89 0-6-0 is used on the Fort Ness branch for shunting duties. The cast metal body mounted on a Minitrix chassis.*

Construction of the baseboard and scenery follows conventional methods. Extensive use of lichen has been made in the modelling of realistic vegetation. The track in the visible section of the layout is all Peco, whereas in the hidden sidings, various makes of points are fitted so that they can be tried out. The structures include both card and plastic kit models. The card kits are from the Hambling's Bilteezi and Highfield ranges, while there are plastic kits from Pola and Vaupe. The signal box, footbridge and some of the road vehicles are old Lone Star models which have been repainted. Other road vehicles are by Wiking and the human figures are Peco and Merten models.

A realistic feature of the layout is the very effective backdrop made up by combining suitable pictures from various calendars. Careful selection, positioning and matching of these pictures together with skilful blending of the modelled scenery with the flat background has given a very realistic impression of depth to the scene. The backdrop conceals the remainder of the oval and the fiddle yard.

Market Redwing

This Great Western layout in TT gauge depicts a small but busy terminus in an imaginary location somewhere between Plymouth and Exeter, but off the main line—access being by single line. There are two branch lines from

Market Redwing, one to Castle Deeping and the other to Cory Bay which is a small seaside town. This arrangement enables a branch line train to travel between Castle Deeping and Cory Bay with Market Redwing being the junction in the middle.

Traffic on the line is typical of that seen in a West Country market town with a Cattle Special from Exeter and a Milk Train from Cory Bay which works through to London. On the passenger side there is *The Coryman Express* which journeys to London daily. An overnight-sleeper-parcels train from Carlisle also works into Market Redwing and this is returned at the end of the day's operations. To complete the passenger service a stopping train from Plymouth also arrives which includes a parcels van for a through working to Cory Bay.

The period modelled is just after nationalisation in the 1948-50 period although Great Western motifs are evident on locomotives and rolling stock. The layout was built with exhibitions in mind and it has appeared at numerous shows. It was designed so that when not in use the layout sections can be stored on racks in a large cupboard. Baseboard construction is of the open frame type using 2 inch by 1 inch timber while pieces of floorboard form the base for the trackwork. The track is Wrenn, glued to a cork strip and, while the glue is still wet, granulated chippings are sprinkled over the complete area. Once dry the surplus is swept away giving a realistic effect. The point work is

Keith Gowen's TT-gauge Market Redwing layout. (Not to scale.)

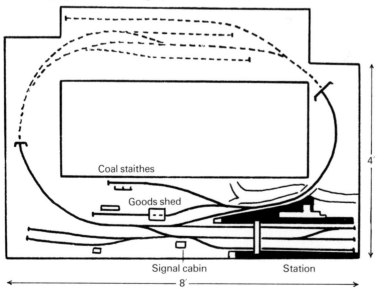

Coal staithes

Goods shed

Signal cabin   Station

4'

8'

Left *A branch line goods train approaches Market Redwing station with the cattle dock to the left and the carriage sidings on the right.*

Below *The approach to Market Redwing station showing the Wrenn pointwork. The signal cabin and goods shed are made up from Hambling's Bilteezi sheets. Note the token exchange apparatus in the left foreground.*

Right *Market Redwing junction station on Keith Gowen's TT scale Great Western layout. The station buildings are from Bilteezi card kits and the footbridge is a modified Triang product.*

dealt with in a similar manner with a copper-clad sleeper replacing the original tie bar; this together with loop wiring gives trouble free operation. The scenery was mostly made from chicken wire covered with Mod-Roc and painted. Some areas have coloured flock sprinkled over glue to give a textured effect.

The working signals are a feature of the layout and were constructed from Bec kits with 3 mm Society signal arms. They are operated by piano wire passing through copper tubing. The level crossing also works and is made from a combination of wood and plastic pieces together with some parts from the Airfix 00-scale level crossing kit. These operating features are popular at exhibitions.

The buildings are mainly constructed from Hambling's Bilteezi printed card kits suitably modified for the situation. For example, the

goods shed was made up from parts from several sheets of the 00 scale Warehouse/School/Narrow Gauge Locomotive Shed kit with Airfix Engine Shed windows. The station platforms are built from balsa wood covered with brickpaper while fine sandpaper was used for the top surfaces. The rolling stock is basically Triang although various Ian Kirk and 3 mm Society products are beginning to replace the Triang vehicles. The locomotives are of Triang origin with kit-built bodies and are all super detailed to give a more realistic effect.

When exhibited the layout operates on an hourly programme which gives a complete day's operations, and there is a card system which indicates to the public just what moves are taking place. Control is with a Hammant & Morgan Clipper controller and self isolating points. The programme cannot be smoothly

run unless the fiddle yard sidings ae operated efficiently and a comprehensive work list is drawn up for this purpose. Thus both the operator and the fiddle sidings assistant know exactly what is going to happen next ensuring straightforward operation. The programme has been designed so that all the trains appear to run for a reason and to be earning revenue, not just aimlessly going round and round a circuit.

Unterlenningen

Unterlenningen is a typical model German branch line terminus in N gauge and it again illustrates the advantages of this small scale in enabling an interesting station to be modelled in a minimum of space. Though the terminus has sufficient facilities to permit entertaining operation it only occupies a baseboard 60 inches by 20 inches. The branch line and terminus are designed to form part of a larger main line layout with a junction station at a later date, but can be operated in the meantime with a fiddle yard. The period has been set to allow the use of both steam and diesel power and facilities for refuelling both have been provided at the terminus together with a combined engine shed and workshop building.

Baseboard construction follows conventional methods with chipboard braced by timber framing; with the relatively narrow baseboard and the strong top surface of chipboard, 1 inch by 1 inch wood was considered sufficient for the framing rather than the more usual 2 inch by 1 inch material. On this surface there are two hidden tracks which will form part of the main line. Above them is supported a further sheet of chipboard on which Unterlenningen station is constructed. Track

Track plan for Unterlenningen, an N-scale German branch line terminus.

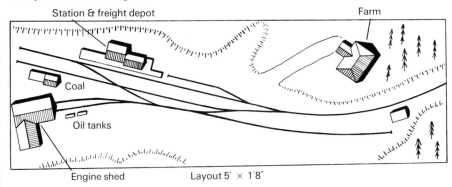

Left *A German prototype branch line terminus in N scale. The layout section illustrated here measures only 60 inches by 20 inches showing how little space is required for branch line modelling in this scale.*

Below left *Unterlenningen Station was built from a Kibri kit. The short passenger train is headed by a Fleischmann model of a German Federal Railways Class BR 91 0-6-0 Tank Engine. This small locomotive is ideal for branch line use.*

and points are from the Arnold range and are ballasted with cork granules. The structures are all made from plastic kits from Pola and Kibri. An excellent range of realistic structure model kits from German prototypes in N scale is available from these and other manufacturers and the kits are readily obtained in this country. The landscape was shaped with thin plywood formers supporting plaster bandage material.

Over this there is a covering of Polyfilla which has been painted appropriately. Scenic dressings applied over this give the surface a realistic texture. Cork bark has been used for cliff faces and rocks and the bushes are of lichen. Numerous commercial tree models of the 'bottle brush' type give a realistic conifer forest effect. Even though the individual trees are simple models the massed appearance is very good. Road vehicles are from the excellent Wiking range. At present the layout is lacking in human figures but these will shortly be added using Preiser and Merten models.

The locomotives and rolling stock are all ready-to-run commercial models mainly from the Arnold and Fleischmann ranges, which include a good selection of smaller locomotives, steam and diesel prototype, suitable for branch line use. Operation follows conventional patterns but the area is assumed to be popular with tourists in the summer thus creating extra passenger traffic.

Layout ideas

To complete this book I would like to look briefly at three branch lines which are still very much operational today to see how we might use each as the basis for a layout. The lines are interesting in appearance and operation as they are now, but if one prefers there is nothing to stop us turning back the clock to steam days while still using information and ideas from these branches. All three are within fairly easy reach of my home showing that it can be worthwhile looking around the area in which you live when seeking a suitable prototype. Each has unusual and interesting features and only one was operated by the Great Western, the other two being Southern lines, showing that there are alternatives to the typical GWR branch line model!

The Weymouth Harbour Tramway

The Weymouth Harbour Tramway is a single track branch which winds its way along for a mile in the streets of Weymouth from the main Weymouth station to the quay. The line was opened for passengers in 1880 and was jointly owned by the London & South Western Railway and the Great Western Railway but was operated by the GWR. For many years the line was worked by a variety of small tank engines but now boat trains from Waterloo (Southern Region) are hauled through to the

quay by main line diesel locomotives. Today it is a remarkable sight on a busy summer day with the streets teeming with holiday visitors and crowded with parked cars to see a boat train slowly rumbling along preceded by police and railwaymen checking that the track is not obstructed. On one side there is the harbour with many small boats, on the other side of the street there are buildings including shops, warehouses, pubs and so on, many of which would be very attractive in model form and which are very suitable for modelling in low relief. At one point a street is carried across the harbour on a bridge which also spans the road along which the track runs.

I have drawn up a plan based on the Weymouth Harbour Tramway for an along-the-wall layout measuring 10 feet by 1½ feet in 00 gauge. The track layout at the terminus is fairly typical of branch line station designs with a run-around loop at the passenger platform and with sidings serving, in this case, the quayside and warehouses at the rear. I have also included a small engine shed with coal and water. However, the choice of prototype does have advantages over the usual country branch line terminus both in the setting and in the operational possibilities. Instead of the usual simple scenic setting this layout has a crowded town scene around the line providing great scope for the modeller who enjoys making

Right *Weymouth Harbour Tramway with a boat train on its way from the quay towards Weymouth station. Note the rails inset into the roadway and the bell mounted on the front of the locomotive above the coupling.*

Below *Track plan for an 00-gauge branch line terminus layout inspired by the Weymouth Harbour Tramway.*

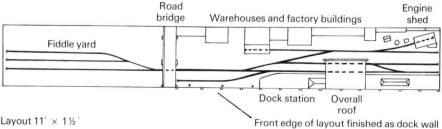

Road bridge   Warehouses and factory buildings   Engine shed

Fiddle yard

Dock station   Overall roof

Layout 11′ × 1½′

Front edge of layout finished as dock wall

Layout ideas

Above *The boat train at Ferry's Corner showing the congested surroundings.*

Left *This fish merchants store is typical of the buildings along the quay. The buildings could be very effectively modelled in low relief on a narrow layout.*

Right *A through train crosses the viaduct as it returns from Lymington Pier station to Lymington Town station.*

buildings and adding small details such as human figures, road vehicles, lamps, street signs and so on. For the best effect the low relief structures at the rear should be based on actual prototypes. The front of the layout can be modelled to represent the edge of the quay giving a very neat and finished appearance and I have used the road bridge as a scenic break to conceal the entrance to the fiddle yard at the left. The station platform is at the edge of the quay so that passengers can go directly up the gangways onto the ferries. I have sketched in an overall roof covering part of the platform and the two tracks.

The layout could be modelled for either steam or diesel operation, the coal and water facilities at the small engine shed being replaced by a diesel fuel oil tank for the latter. Operation can be interesting with passenger trains arriving to connect with ferry sailings and these trains can include main line coaches; if more space is available for the layout the platform and run-around loop could be lengthened with benefit, as at present only short trains can be run. A small steam or diesel shunting locomotive can be employed sorting wagons and vans and shunting them onto the appropriate sidings.

Lymington

This 4½-mile long branch leaves the main Southampton-Bournemouth line at Lymington Junction, 1 mile west of Brockenhurst and runs to Lymington Town and Lymington Pier. The branch to the Town station was opened in 1858 by the Lymington Railway Company and was taken over 20 years later by the London & South Western Railway. This company extended the branch another ½ mile from the Town station to reach the Pier. The regular ferry service from Lymington Pier to the Isle of Wight has provided a great deal of traffic for the branch and has ensured its survival despite the many closures which have taken place elsewhere. The branch was steam operated until 1967 when it was electrified and it is now worked by electric multiple units (EMUs). The run-around loops and sidings at both Lymington Town and Lymington Pier stations have been removed leaving only the single line and, although the branch is still interesting in appearance, operation is limited in scope even though there are hourly trains for much of the day. I have based my suggested layout on the early 1960s when the track layouts were more interesting, giving more operational possibilities. An excellent book on the line, *The*

Lymington Town station is an attractive structure and would make an interesting model. Unfortunately the impressive train shed which covered part of the platform and the platform track has been removed.

Above *Lymington Pier signal cabin is a small brick-built structure which faces out across the river. Note the 'W' (whistle) sign for trains approaching the viaduct. The cabin was built in the 1950s.*
Below *Lymington Pier station with its distinctive curved canopy.*

Layout ideas

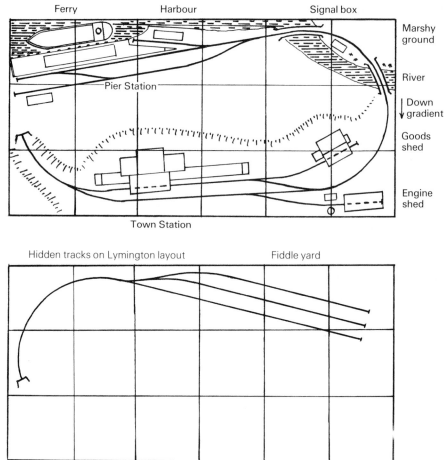

Ferry   Harbour   Signal box

Marshy ground

River

Down gradient

Goods shed

Engine shed

Pier Station

Town Station

Hidden tracks on Lymington layout   Fiddle yard

Lymington Branch by P. Paye (The Oakwood Press), has recently been published and the author includes sketches of the track plans at various periods together with a great deal of other information on the branch.

Although the layout could be of the usual along the wall or L shape in the corner of the room type I recalled a layout plan I had seen some years ago in *Model Railway News,* with a terminus and a through station on a rectangular baseboard with the track leading to a fiddle yard beneath the terminus. The design seemed an ideal basis for this layout and I have used this arrangement but have based the stations on the Lymington Town and Pier prototypes. It was necessary to alter the position of the goods shed at the former and to omit most of the sidings there but the Pier station is essentially similar to the real one.

The layout has attractive scenic possibilities with the river and harbour, complete with

Track plan for a layout based on Lymington.

ferry. The Skinley range of blueprints includes a small car ferry which, though smaller than the ferries used on the Lymington to Isle of Wight run, would be an attractive addition to the scene. If you wish, a row of houses, together with the Railway Hotel, can be placed behind the Town station. Along the centre of the layout a ridge of hills or a double-sided backdrop would scenically separate the two sides of the layout and give a greater impression of distance between the two stations. Operational scope will be rather greater than for the usual terminus to fiddle yard design because of the additional through station at which extra train movements can take place. The layout is designed for 00 gauge in an area of 6 feet by 3 feet but could be built in N gauge in a correspondingly smaller space.

Hamworthy Goods Branch

This line has an interesting history. It branches from the old Southampton & Dorchester Railway at Hamworthy Junction and serves what was the original Poole station, on the west side of the harbour. This station was opened in 1847 and in about 1860 the single track of the branch was doubled. However trafic on the line became less as further lines were built and the present Poole station in the centre of the town was opened in 1872. The line was closed to passengers in 1896 and was singled again but is still open for freight. The station became Hamworthy Goods but the building is now derelict. However the line is still busy with the yard shunted daily, usually by a Class 33 locomotive and with a daily Freightliner train to Southampton. There are also Cartic trains carrying imported cars to the Midlands. The branch serves the Lower Hamworthy wharves and industrial area. Industries here include a coal yard, oil depots, ship repair slipway, yacht builder, sand and gravel hoppers, cement hoppers and an engineering works.

My plan inspired by the Hamworthy Branch is for an L-shaped layout with a fiddle yard concealed by low relief structures at the right-hand end. From these hidden sidings trains arrive at the run-around loop and the stock is then shunted onto the appropriate sidings serving various industries. There are sufficient of these to make for interesting operation particularly if one of the card order schemes for deciding on the destinations for the rolling stock is employed. The lap point at the right-hand end of the run-around loop is typical in industrial yards and the one at Lower Hamworthy is shown in one of the photographs. For 00-gauge points of this type are available commercially from Piko and Fleischmann; they are equivalent to a right-hand and a left-hand point combined and occupy less space than two separate points. Curves on the layout are of small radius but this is typical of industrial and dockside areas and they will cause no problems with the small locomotives

The coal wharf at Lower Hamworthy with the Ruston & Hornsby diesel shunting coal wagons.

Layout ideas

Industries in Lower Hamworthy include **(above)** a fuel oil depot; **(below)** a ship repair yard; **(above right)** a gravel hopper; **(right and below right)** the coal wharf and depot. All of these can be modelled effectively.

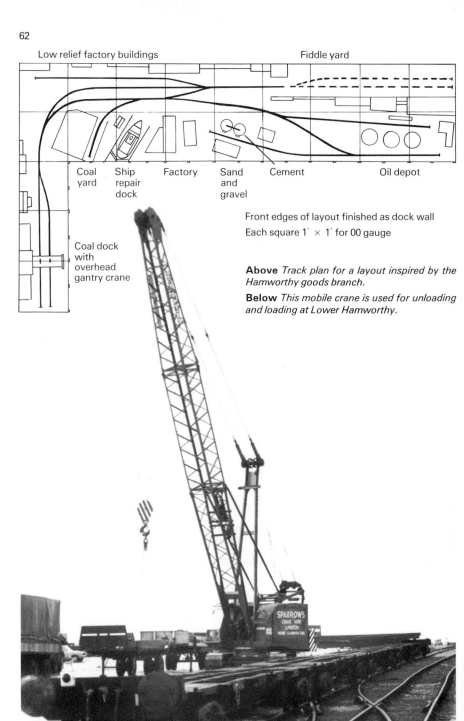

Low relief factory buildings   Fiddle yard

Coal   Ship   Factory   Sand   Cement   Oil depot
yard   repair   and
        dock   gravel

Coal dock
with
overhead
gantry crane

Front edges of layout finished as dock wall

Each square 1′ × 1′ for 00 gauge

Above *Track plan for a layout inspired by the Hamworthy goods branch.*

Below *This mobile crane is used for unloading and loading at Lower Hamworthy.*

Top *Complex pointwork at Lower Hamworthy includes a lap point at the left of the picture. The tracks are not all still in use.*

Above *The Fleischmann range of HO-scale track includes this lap point useful for cramped situations, for example, in industrial areas.*

suitable for shunting on this layout. For enthusiasts who enjoy shunting, operation on the layout will offer considerable scope. Though the prototype carries only freight traffic, the modeller could run a few trains for the workmen giving the opportunity for some limited passenger traffic. The variety of industries served enables a wide range of rolling stock to be justifiably run on the layout, including some special types if desired. There is a good selection of ready-to-run and cast metal kit locomotives, both steam and diesel prototypes, which will be suitable for the line.

Scenically the scope of the layout is almost unlimited with numerous interesting industrial buildings to be constructed and with many small details which can be added to the area around the tracks. There are some excellent plastic kits for oil tanks, cement hoppers, cranes and other industrial structures made by Kibri, Faller, Vollmer and other manufacturers. Though strictly these are HO rather than 00 scale most of these models will look realistic on an 00-gauge layout. The ship repair slipway is an interesting feature and well worth including on a layout. The ship model can be scratch-built, perhaps following one of the Skinley blueprints, or you can adapt one of the plastic kit models on the market. The front edge of the layout can be finished to look like the wall of the dock giving a very realistic effect. At the rear of the layout low relief buildings give an impression of depth and completeness. Behind this only a sky blue backdrop will be needed.

Layout ideas

Above *This 00 scale Johnson 0-4-0 was constructed from a K's kit. It would be ideal for a small industrial branch line.*

Below *Graham Bailey modelled this realistic dock scene in N scale. The ship model is the Novo Shell Welder.*